Divorce

Redefining the Terms of the Debate

Lenard Marlow

Book Vine Press
2516 Highland Dr.
Palatine, IL 60067

CONTENTS

PREFACE

If you have read the first two books about divorce in this series, *A Common Sense, Practical Guide To Divorce* and *Divorce: Accepting Imperfect Solutions To Imperfect Problems,* you know that their principal message is that we do not live in a world of possible perfection. Rather, we live in a very imperfect world, one of inevitable constraint and human limitation. In a sense, that was also true of the first book in this series, *The Book About Marriage: Entering It, Sustaining It, Ending It.* I never suggested that, after reading that book, men and women would give up the idea of romantic marriage and stop falling in love. Far more modestly, my hope was that they would be more conscious of the effect that the forces that were motivating their decision-making process were having on them.

The same was true when it came to the first two books in this series about divorce. I wanted to put to rest the suggestion that turning to the law for help would not only answer all of the questions and solve all of the problems that husbands and wives found themselves faced with as a result of their decision to divorce, but also give them the right answers and solutions, whatever that meant. Nevertheless, I pretty much left it at that. To be sure, I introduced the idea of viewing the law as a common *framework* that divorcing husbands and wives could turn to in their effort to conclude an agreement rather than, as a divorce lawyer viewed and employed the law, as a weapon in a legal tug of war the object of which was simply to get as much as you could and to give as little as you had to. Nevertheless, I still left the law as being somewhat at the center of a divorcing husband's and wife's world.

Increasingly, I had a problem with that. After all, my thesis was that husbands and wives should make the decisions in their divorce on the same basis that they had made them in their marriage, and they certainly hadn't made them by looking to the law. As a result, after I finished writing that second book on divorce, and just before I submitted it for publication, I went back and added a new chapter, Chapter 16, An Assumption of Risk An Assumption of Responsibility. The addition of that chapter changed the name of the game and, in turn, the terms of the debate. Rather than looking to the law with the expectation that it would provide all of the answers to their questions and solutions to their problems, divorcing husbands and wives would now be charged with the responsibility of looking more to themselves for those answers and solutions.

But there was another reason why I introduced that idea. As I said, for me the most important new idea that I had introduced into the conversation was that, rather than view the law as a weapon in a legal tug of war, as a divorce lawyer did, the far better and more responsible way to view the law was as a common *framework* that divorcing husbands and wives could look to in their effort to conclude an agreement which, without thinking about it, was how I and the people with whom I worked had unconsciously always viewed and employed the law. And that is how I presented the law in the first two books on divorce in this series.

Nevertheless, once that second book on divorce was published, I again found myself feeling uncomfortable. To be sure, I felt that the introduction of the idea of an assumption of risk and an assumption of responsibility was not only a very important contribution to the discussion but in many ways the missing piece. But I still felt that I had not sufficiently underscored why looking to the law was not enough— why it could not answer all of a divorcing husband's and wife's questions and solve all of their problem. That is when I came up with the idea of this last book in the series, which I did not even start writing until the first three books in the series (and the Workbook that is a companion to the first book on divorce) were already published.

Thus, as is the case with Chapter 16 in the second book on divorce in this series, this last book is also really an afterthought. Having said that, I have to add something. I like to think that I have introduced many ideas into the discussion that have never been introduced before. I also like to think that, though they are at variance with, and take exception to, literally all of the conventional wisdom in the field, I have been able to express them in such a way that, when I get through, what I have said seems nothing more than common sense. That being so, all that you will need is an open mind.

I have to add two last things. Despite the fact that this is the shortest book in the series, I would argue that it is the most important. As I said, it is intended to change the very terms of the debate. Nevertheless, when you get through reading it, hopefully you will see that what I am proposing is not really revolutionary at all. If it is no more than common sense, as I like to believe that it is, how could it be? In the terms that I have put it throughout this series, it was just the picture that held you captive that disabled you from being able to see it.

This brings me to the last thing that I have to say by way of introduction. As the title of this book suggests, its purpose is to change the terms of the debate. Unfortunately, that is far easier said than done, as I learned when I sat down to do that. My answer, which I only came up with after I had finished writing the book, was to tell the story in two parts. In Part I, which was originally the book, I will tell it from the standpoint of the current terms of the debate. In Part II, which will consist of just two chapters and a Conclusion, I will tell it from the standpoint of the new terms of the debate that I am proposing.

PART 1

The Current Terms of the Debate

CHAPTER 1

LOOKING TO THE LAW

Whether you turn to divorce lawyers (or collaborative family lawyers) or to a divorce mediator, you will necessarily end up looking to the law. In the past, divorcing husbands and wives looked to the law for a very limited purpose. Their decision to divorce had left them with some unexpected questions that they had to answer and problems that they had to solve and they needed help. And the law was of great help. It not only provided them with answers to their questions and solutions to their problems, but in most instances also left them with clear ones.

That all changed with the sudden, dramatic increase in the rate of divorce that took place in the early 1960's, initially in the United States and western Europe and eventually in most parts of the world. As I said, until then the law in the various states had a rather limited function. Except in community property states, what was his was his and what was hers was hers and what was in their joint names was theirs and would be divided down the middle. And that was basically it. Thus, when divorcing husbands and wives looked to the law, which they did, it was usually for a very limited purpose—for example, to determine the payment that the husband would make to the wife for her support or for the support of their children and for how long. In most other instances, such as with whom their children would live, they already knew the answer. They would continue to live with their mother.

As I said, that all changed with the dramatic changes in our divorce laws that were enacted in response to the tremendous increase in the rate of divorce, which were now referred to as our equitable distribution laws. Those laws were enacted with the specific intention of broadening the reach of the law. More specifically, it was felt that divorce laws which simply left the parties where they were left divorcing wives at a distinct disadvantage. As it was expressed, our existing divorce laws did not adequately take into account the contribution, and in many cases sacrifices, that women had made during the course of their marriage. Thus, the call was to make our divorce laws more equitable. That was the good news. The bad news was that it also made the application of our divorce laws far more complicated and, therefore, more difficult to apply. That was because divorcing husbands and wives now found themselves faced with far more questions that they had to answer and problems that they had to solve than had previously been the case. Worse, they were far harder to answer or solve. In the terms that I will put it, it put far more weight on our divorce laws than they could bear.

Unfortunately, as quickly became apparent, that left divorcing husbands and wives with a much bigger problem. That problem was that those they turned to for help, principally divorce lawyers and divorce mediators, had very different views when it came to the question of why divorcing husbands and wives were looking to the law and what they could expect of it. (Since, as I have argued, most divorce mediators are simply divorce lawyers dressed in sheep's clothing, that was not really the case. But it will not get us anywhere to go into that, at least now.)

This brings me to what I have argued in the books about divorce in this series are the critical questions, ones that had never really been asked before, at least not in the terms that I have posed them. How did those who were advising divorcing husbands and wives at this critical time view the law and, to the extent that they were directing its application, how were they employing it? More to the point, when it comes to the redefinition of the terms of the debate that I am calling for, did their approach to the law leave divorcing husbands and wives with better and clearer answers to their questions and solutions to their problems or, as I am going to argue, was that just so much irresponsible pie in the sky.

For the purposes of the discussion that follows, I am going to look to the legal rules (laws) that divorce lawyers (and collaborative family lawyers) insist that husbands and wives in the state of New York must employ in their attempt to conclude an agreement. And the question I will pose is whether the strict application of those rules will enable them both to get it done and to get it right, as divorce lawyers claim, or whether that is just their conceit—in my terms. just so much legal nonsense. And if I am turning to New York's divorce laws, it is not because they better serve my purpose. It is simply because, having practiced in New York all of my professional life, I am most familiar with them.

With that in mind I will now turn to New York's divorce laws (Equitable Distribution Laws). While they are obviously different than the divorce laws in other states (for example a child is deemed emancipated at 18 in California, but not until 21 in New York), for our purposes there is no significance in that difference any more than there is in the fact that the age at which a child can obtain a license to drive a car is also different from state to state. In fact, it would be more appropriate to view those differences as being just different customs or rules of the road. To be sure, a divorce lawyer will take exception to that suggestion. That is because it better serves his purpose to characterize our divorce laws as representing a husband's and wife's *legal rights*. Otherwise, why would it be so important to look to them, let alone sanctify and champion them? Again, a coin would do as well.

CHAPTER 2

DIVORCE LAWYERS

As I pointed out in the first book on divorce in this series, *A Common Sense, Practical Guide To Divorce,* from the standpoint of a divorce lawyer or a collaborative family lawyer, divorcing husbands and wives will turn to the law for three reasons. First, because their decision to divorce has left them with a legal problem, namely, that of securing their legal rights. Second, because doing so will answer the questions and solve the problems that their decision to divorce has left them with, thereby enabling then to get it done. Third, because measuring the agreement they have concluded against the yardstick provided by the law will assure them that they have been left with the right answers to their questions and solutions to their problems—as I will put it, that they got it right.

To be sure, they could employ a coin for that purpose. But no one would suggest that flipping a coin would get it right. And that, of course, is a divorce lawyer's and a collaborative family lawyer's objection to divorce mediation. As is the case with those who resort to a coin, a divorce mediator is only interested in getting it done, not in getting it right.

It is not necessary for me to repeat my answer to this when it comes to a divorce lawyer, namely, that his (or her) goal is not to get it right, whatever that means. It is simply to get as much as he can and to give as little as he has to, and all of the rest is just so much talk. Nor is it necessary to point out that, unlike the rules of mathematics, which are the same everywhere and at all times, the legal rules that a divorce lawyer looks to and employs do not satisfy either of those requirements, which is why a coin would do as well. But I am not going to press that point. Rather, for the sake of the argument, in the discussion that follows I will assume that, like the rules of mathematics, legal rules are the same everywhere and at all times—in other words, that they are universal.

Unfortunately, that still leaves us with a problem. Unlike the rules of mathematics, the application of legal rules will not leave you with an answer, to the eighth decimal point if necessary. With rare exception, such as the age at which a child is emancipated, all that it will leave you with is a range of possible answers.

In and of itself, a range of possible answers would not stand in the way of a divorcing husband and wife being able to conclude an agreement. If there is a range, they could simply split it down the middle. The problem is that when divorcing husbands and wives make the mistake of turning to divorce lawyers whose sole interest is in getting as much as they can and giving as little as they have to, it is in the very nature of the application of legal rules that the range of possible answers that they will be given will be so large that it will not serve as a common *framework* that they can look to in their effort to conclude an agreement. Rather, looking to the range of possible answers provided by the law will only make it that much harder if not impossible. But I am going to put it more directly. Looking to the law will not solve the problem as divorce lawyers would have it. Looking to the law as divorce lawyers do will actually create the problem.

And that, of course, has been the fate of divorcing husbands and wives who have been encouraged to turn to our adversarial legal system and the divorce lawyers who are its agents to answer their questions and solve their problems. And if they do eventually conclude an agreement, more often than not it is only to avoid leaving it in the hands of the court. After all, since neither of their attorneys knows what the outcome will be, that will only commit them to a crap shoot.

Why have divorcing husbands and wives been left with such a large range of possible answers if that really doesn't serve their interests? Because it serves the interests of divorce lawyers. To make their case, divorce lawyers need as much running room as they can get, and a narrow range of possible answers will not do that. And it makes no difference to divorce lawyers that a narrow range of possible answers would better serve the needs of their clients. As I said in the first book on divorce in this series, that is one of a divorce lawyer's dirty little secrets.

CHAPTER 3

WOMEN'S ADVOCATES

This brings me to the second group that has been most responsible for the shape and content of our current divorce laws. They have also been the ones who are responsible for the fact that our divorce laws have been of so little help. They are women's advocates and organizations such as The National Organization of Women (NOW). But though no one seems to have realized this, they were of no benefit to divorcing wives. They didn't get it right and they didn't get it done. They struck out on both counts.

They certainly did not facilitate getting it done by encouraging divorcing wives to employ the law as a common *framework* that they could look to in an effort to conclude an agreement rather than as a weapon in a legal tug of war. Their insistence that divorcing women had to turn to divorce lawyers rather than to a divorce mediator insured that. But what really put the final nail in the coffin was the provisions that they insisted had to be included in our equitable distribution statutes to compensate divorcing wives for the opportunities they had lost as a result of the contributions they had made to the marriage by staying at home and being a homemaker and mother to their children. As I said, what is most incredible is the fact that, to my knowledge, no one else has ever pointed this out.

To make my case here, I am going to refer to four of the factors that a court in New York is required to consider in determining the amount of maintenance, if any, that the wife is to receive on the income above the income cap. Don't be fooled by the fact that the statute talks about "a party", not "the wife." As the preamble to New York's Equitable Distribution Laws made clear, its provisions were directed to women.

9. The care of children or step-children, disabled adult children or stepchildren, elderly parents or in-laws provided during the marriage that inhibits a party's earning capacity.

12. The reduced or lost earning capacity of the payee as a result of having foregone or delayed education, training, employment or career opportunities during the marriage.

14. The contribution and services of the payee as a spouse, parent, wage earner and homemaker and to the career or career potential of the other party.

15. Any other factor which the court shall expressly find to be just and proper.

Before I turn to those factors, I want to return to the insistence of woman's advocates that a divorcing wife had to turn to a divorce lawyer, and an adversarial legal proceeding, rather than to divorce mediation, to press her claim. As will be clear. that is the most unfortunate mistake a divorcing wife could make. To be sure, turning to an adversarial divorce proceeding, as women's advocates insisted, would guarantee that a divorcing wife would have an advocate by her side to champion her cause. But it would also guarantee that she would now be dealing with a husband who would have one by his side as well. And though woman's advocates did not realize this, that would leave divorcing wives at a distinct disadvantage. Let me explain.

In almost all other instances, though there might be a wide range of possible answers and, therefore, a large difference between a wife's position and her husband's position, there would still be a range of possible answers to work with, hopefully successfully. In this case, however, there will be no such range—absolutely none. And where there is no range of possible answers, there will be nothing for the wife's attorney and the husband's attorney to discuss. How is that possible? It is built into the system and the factors that the court is directed to consider in making its determination.

We know what the wife's advocate will ask for based on those factors—the stars, the moon and the sun. What will the husband's advocate offer in response? Nothing. Absolutely nothing. In fact, it would constitute malpractice for the husband's attorney to do otherwise. Remember, this is not divorce mediation where the husband and the wife are looking to the law to find a common *framework* in aid of their being able to conclude an agreement. This is an adversarial divorce proceeding where the object is to get as much as you can and to give as little as you have to. To be sure, when it comes to the basic amount of maintenance, looking to the law will provide a husband and wife with that common *framework*. In fact, it will provide them with an exact number, to the eighth decimal point if necessary. But not when it comes to the maintenance payment on the income above the income cap. As the statute makes clear, it will be the amount, "if any."

And that will be the husband's attorney's position. There shouldn't be any. As I said, if the statute clearly says, which it does, "if any" (if one of the possibilities is that there will be no payment based on the income above the income cap), there would be no reason for the husband's attorney to offer any and every reason for him not to. Remember, the onus is not on the husband's attorney to prove that there shouldn't be any such payment. The onus is on the wife's attorney to show, first, that there should be such a payment and, second, what the amount of that payment should be. In short, in insisting that divorcing wives must turn to divorce lawyers rather than a divorce mediator, the scales were tipped in favor of the wife's husband.

What will be the result? As I said, the wife's attorney will ask for the moon, the stars and the sun and the husband's attorney won't offer a penny. In short, it will literally be impossible for the husband and wife to conclude an agreement.

I

Won't that leave both the husband and the wife with a problem? Yes and no. Yes, in the sense that since they have not been able to solve their problem, they will have to turn to the court to solve it. No, because this has left the wife at a distinct disadvantage. In fact, it has really left her nowhere.

On the face of it, the matter is now in the court's hands. In other words, the husband and wife will both sit back and leave it to the court to look at the various factors that the statute has directed it to consider in making its decision. But that is not how it really works. If the wife is arguing that the factors enumerated in the statute have left her at a disadvantage, the burden of proof is not on her husband to disprove that. It is on her to prove it. In other words, it is not enough for the wife to claim that she has been left at a disadvantage. She has to prove that if she hadn't stayed at home to be a homemaker, raise their children and take care of their aged and infirm relatives, she could have gone out and, like her husband, pursued a career of her own. To be sure, she might have been able to satisfy her burden of proof even 75 years ago. But she will never be able to do that today. Let me explain.

The factors that the court is directed to look at only come into play if the combined incomes of the parties is above the income cap, which as of March, 2022 was $203,000. Below that, the maintenance payment to be paid by the husband to the wife is based on a strict formula. So, though we would not classify the family here as being rich, we are not talking about a poor or middle-class family either. We are talking about an upper middle-class family.

There are two possibilities here. In one case only the husband is employed, and the income above the income cap is all his. In the other, the husband and wife are both employed, but the husband earns more. But in an upper middle-class family like this, the wife does not wait on tables or clean houses. As we would say, she has a "real" job. She might even be a professional.

Again, that might not have been the case 75 years ago. After all, Harvard Law School did not admit women until 1950. Today, however, more than 50% of Harvard Law School students are women. And that is true across the board—it is the same in medical school as well. But the change is even more dramatic when it comes to attendance in college. Though this was certainly not the case 75 years ago, today women account for almost 60% of college students and men for only a little over 40%.

But there is an even more important factor in the equation. Men and women marry much later today than they did 75 years ago, particularly those who went to college and graduate school. Upper middle-class women today do not marry when they are 21 or 22. They marry when they are in their very late 20's and early 30's. In many cases they marry even later than that. What were they doing all of that time? Like their husbands, pursuing their careers.

That was before they had children. But all of that changed when children came along. No it didn't. To be sure, it may (or may not) have been the case 75 years ago that women stopped working for good once they had children. But that is not the case today, particularly for the women we are talking about. Women today do not go to law school, medical school, or business school after college just to work for 6 or 7 years before they get married and have children. If they were very smart students, they didn't go to college with that in mind. Like their husbands, they pursued a higher education in order to have a successful career of their own. After all, they did not know when, if ever, they would marry. As a result, having worked hard to create a successful career of their own, they will want to hold on to it even after they have children, just on a more limited basis.

Will they be able to do that? The chances are very good that they will. After all, they will not be waiting on tables or cleaning homes. And they will not be applying for a job where no one knows them. They will continue to work where they are, just on a more limited basis. And since the wife has already established a relationship with those with whom she works, they may be very happy to have her continue to work there. Just as important, while this was not the case 75 years ago, today she may even be able to work from home.

II

This brings me back to my original question. Did women's advocates do women any favor by persuading our state legislatures to include provisions, such as the one we are considering, to compensate women for the opportunities they lost as a result of the contributions they made to their marriage by staying at home and being a homemaker and mother to their children?

Up until this point I have rested my case that they didn't on the fact that women today are in a very different position than they were 75 years ago in that they have opportunities that were not available to them then. But that is not the end of the story. Even if the wife can demonstrate that her obligations as a wife, home maker and mother severely limited her ability to be gainfully employed and to establish a career of her own, for which reason she should receive all or a portion of her husband's income above the income cap, the husband's attorney will still not offer her a penny. Why not?Because the burden of proof here is on the wife and she will never be able to meet it.

To be sure, the statute provides that, in determining the amount of maintenance, if any, that the wife is to receive on the income above the income cap, the court is required to consider the reduced or lost earning capacity of the payee (in this case the wife) as a result of having foregone or delayed education, training, employment or career opportunities during the marriage. And that seems to assign the obligation to determine whether that is so to the court. But, as the husband's attorney knows, that is not the case. All that the court (the trial judge) is going to do is sit back and listen to the evidence presented by the wife to support that conclusion to determine whether the wife has made her case—in legal terms, sustained her burden of proof. And the husband's attorney knows that she will never be able to do that.

To be sure, the wife will be able to make a convincing argument that she forfeited or delayed education, training, employment and career opportunities during the marriage. But that only meets half of her burden of proof. It doesn't meet the other half, which is to establish her lost or reduced earning capacity. How can the court (the trial judge) make an appropriate determination if it does not know that? It can't.

Suppose that the wife's attorney, in order to meet the wife's burden of proof, asks the wife what would have been her goal had she not been deprived of the opportunity to pursue it. Suppose, further, that the wife testifies that her dream was to go to law school, work hard, get a law degree, study and pass the bar examination, secure a position at a prominent law firm in the community, eventually become a partner, and enjoy a successful and financially rewarding career until she retired.

Now the wife has met her burden of proof. No she hasn't. Her testimony didn't prove a thing. It was just so much pie in the sky. As the husband's lawyer will demonstrate on cross-examination, the wife does not and cannot know whether she would have been admitted to law school, whether she would have graduated, whether she would have passed the bar examination and been offered a job at a prominent law firm in the community, what she would have earned or whether she would have ever become a partner in the firm. In short, the wife's testimony did not constitute proof. It was only wishful thinking, which is why the undertaking was pointless. As the husband's attorney knew, you cannot prove something that never happened.

That is why women's advocates didn't do divorcing wives any favor when they pressured our state legislatures to include all of those factors into the equation and persuade divorcing wives to turn to divorce lawyers rather than to divorce mediation. Look how long it took and how much it cost for them to go nowhere.

III

There was yet another problem here which women's advocates who urged divorcing wives to turn to divorce lawyers didn't take into account. Let us assume that the wife is able to meet her burden of proof. In fact, let us assume that she is able to demonstrate to the court's satisfaction that her loss is equal to most if not all of the husband's income above the income cap. Will the court award her most if not all of her husband's income above the income cap? No.

The hard and intractable reality is that the pie is just so big. And it doesn't get any bigger because the wife's and children's legitimate needs get bigger. I made that point in a previous book in this series when, in referring to the percentage of the husband's income that the wife would receive in child support, I said that it was 17% for one child, 25% for two and only 4% more for the third and 2% more for the fourth and asked, "What, do the third and fourth child eat less?"

It doesn't make any difference. The husband has to receive an appropriate portion of that pie as well, and if he doesn't there is the danger that he may not hang around very long. And all of the wonderful provisions that women's advocates were able to induce our state's legislatures to include for their benefit didn't change that. Needless to say, those who encouraged divorcing wives to turn to divorce lawyers rather than to divorce mediation didn't tell them this.

Am I suggesting that divorcing wives will do better, let alone get what they are asking for, if they turn to divorce mediation? Absolutely not. How do I know that? Besides, is the fact that the pie is only so big any less true in mediation? I am not even going to bring up the fact that it would certainly be a far less time consuming and expensive undertaking if they did. Rather, I will go back to what is the principal message of this series of books, namely, that one cannot expect perfect solutions to imperfect problems. And those who hold out that possibility to divorcing wives (or their husbands) are not doing them any favor.

IV

Up until this point I have been talking about upper middle-class families where the husband earns between $150,000 and $175,000 per year. What about those families where, though not rich in the sense of being worth several million dollars, the husband earns between $450,000 and $550,000 a year? Don't wives in marriages such as this need the benefit of those factors? Not really. The object, at least at this point, is not to ensure that a divorcing husband or wife will be able to live exactly as they did in the past. It is to assure that they will be able to live essentially as they did in the past. To be sure, they may not be able to take an expensive vacation each year as they customarily did. But that does not mean that they will not be able to live essentially as they did in the past. It just means that some small compromises will have to be made. We have a name for that. It is called life. Besides, this is only for today. For most divorcing couples, tomorrow, which will or may be different, may also be a little better.

But what about families that, by any standard, are very rich? I didn't say billionaires. I am talking about a situation where the family's net worth, exclusive of the equity in their home, is $30 million or more in today dollars. That is not a problem. That is because the provisions of our equitable distribution statutes dealing with awards of maintenance do not apply to them. They only apply in those situations where maintenance is applicable, and maintenance is not applicable where a husband and wife will be dividing $30 million or more. I will return to this at a later point.

CHAPTER 4

THE ACADEMIC LEGAL COMMUNITY

This brings me to the third group which has been responsible for the fact that our divorce laws have been such a failure in enabling those who look to the law for help to get answers to their questions and solutions to their problems—in the terms that I have put it, to use the law as a common *framework* rather than as a weapon in a legal tug of war. That is the academic legal community.

On the face of it, it will be hard to understand how I could accuse the academic legal community of doing anything. After all, all that they are doing is sitting on the sidelines and observing the undertaking. That is my indictment. They are just sitting on the sidelines doing nothing but observing the undertaking. And, as I am going to argue, it is disgraceful.

As I did in a previous book of mine, *Divorce: The Conflict Between Getting It Right and Getting It Done*, and as I did again in Chapter 11 of one of the previous books in this series, *Divorce: Accepting Imperfect Solutions To Imperfect Problems*, I called for what I referred to as a Copernican revolution in the law. At the present time, the law, like the sun, is at the center of our legal universe and it is for divorcing husbands and wives to align their efforts to conclude an agreement within the shadow that it casts over their discussions The purpose of my proposed Copernican revolution in the law was to reverse that and place a divorcing husband's and wife's efforts to conclude an agreement, rather than the sun (the law), at the center of our legal universe. In terms of the conflict between getting it right and getting it done, when it comes to any proposed new divorce law, the question our state legislatures should ask is not whether the shadow it will cast over a divorcing couple's efforts to conclude an agreement will enable them to get it right. (As I hope the previous books in this series have made clear, it is not possible for the law to get it right, whatever that means.) It will be to ask whether it will enable divorcing husbands and wives to get it done.

To make my point I referred to a law review article that was published many years ago by Professors Robert H. Mnookin and Lewis Kornhauser entitled *Bargaining in the Shadow of the Law—The Case of Divorce,* which, as I learned, was the most often cited law review article that had ever been published. Why was it so often cited? Aside from making the point that the law was at the center of a divorcing husband's and wife's legal universe, the article didn't say anything. Not a thing. Having made that point, the authors simply stopped.

What was going on here? It was really very simple. This was at a time when the ADR (alternative means of dispute resolution) movement was coming on the scene and there were those committed to our adversarial legal system who were worried about its implications—where it was taking us. (After all, it was not referred to as an alternate means of problem solving.) I am not suggesting that Professors Mnookin's and Kornhauser's purpose was to assuage the concerns of those in the academic legal community who were worried about where it was taking us. I am just saying that there is no other explanation as to why this law review article was so often cited. It didn't say anything. And that wasn't because members of the academic legal community were not in the habit of commenting on and making suggestions when it came to proposed reforms in our laws. That was one of their functions.

But it goes further than that. Professors Mnookin and Kornhauser made it very clear that the law, not a divorcing couple's efforts to conclude an agreement, was to be at the center of a divorcing husband's and wife's universe and, as such, it was for them to align their efforts to conclude an agreement with the shadow that the law cast over their discussions. As I said in *Divorce: Accepting Imperfect Solutions to Imperfect Problems*:

"Having established the law as the center of a husband's and wife's universe, did they propose even a single change in our divorce laws to make them a better instrument than they presently are to aid husbands and wives who look to the law for guidance to get answers to their question? The answer is no."

Even if Professors Mnookin and Kornhauser did not believe, as I do, that an adversarial divorce proceeding is an irresponsible approach to a divorcing husband's and wife's problems, did they really believe that it was perfect and therefore could not be made better? Were they so held captive by their own picture of divorce, which placed the law, like the sun, at the center of a divorcing couple's universe, that it never occurred to them to ask the question that my proposed Copernican revolution in the law insisted was the essential one? Having secured our divorce laws as the center of their universe, thereby reinforcing our adversarial legal system's characterization of the law as representing the parties' *legal rights*, did they really believe that there was nothing further that had to be said?

To be sure, from time to time they admitted that the law did not cast a very clear shadow over the parties' discussions. Thus, as they acknowledged:

"Legal rules are generally not...simple or straight-forward.... Often the outcome in court is far from certain, with any number of outcomes possible. Indeed, existing legal standards governing custody, alimony, child support, and marital property are all striking for their lack of precision and thus provide a bargaining background clouded by uncertainty."

It cannot be emphasized too strongly how significant that last statement is. Professors Mnookin and Kornhauser acknowledged everything that I have been saying in all of the books in this series, namely, that our divorce laws are doing a terrible disservice to the husbands and wives who look to the law for help. Our divorce laws are compounding the problems that they are faced with rather than being of any assistance to them. But having done that, Professors Mnookin and Kornhausei did not raise a finger—not a single finger—to help them. Nor, of course, did the organized matrimonial legal community. Divorce lawyers just continued to take advantage of the gift that our state legislators had given to them which, with Professors Mnookin's and Kornhauser's blessing, they continued to employ to the detriment of the husbands and wives that they represented. As we say, there ought to be a law.

CHAPTER 5

PRINCIPLE

Until this point, my critique of our divorce laws has been focused on two things. The first, which has been principally directed at divorce lawyers, is their use of the law as a weapon in a legal tug of war the object of which is simply to get as much as you can and to give as little as you have to. The second, which has been principally directed at women's advocates, is their attempt to use the law as a means of repaying to women what they sacrificed in becoming wives to their husbands and mothers to their children.

My present critique is a little different but, I would argue, just as important. But unlike all of the factors that go into the equation when it comes to those other issues, it is isn't dependent on any factor at all. It is based on principle, in this case the principle that equitable is equal. To be sure, we do not refer to our divorce laws as being *equal* divorce laws. We refer to them as being *equitable* divorce laws. But, from its earliest days, those on the receiving end (but not on the giving end) viewed them as such. There was also a natural tendency to equate them. You could define an equal division. How could you define an equitable division? You couldn't.

To make my point, I will relate a conversation that I had with a good friend of mine. After a very successful experience at law school (he was first in his class) he joined and eventually became a partner in the largest law firm in his city and one of the largest in the country. He also became the President of his state's Bar Association. He specialized as a divorce lawyer and had a national reputation.

On this occasion he related a case in which he was currently involved. It was really a very simple matter. The couple had been married for a very long time and their children were all grown. They had a net worth of $230 million, which was all in the husband's name and which, since it was all acquired during their marriage, was marital property. It was literally a one issue matter. How was that $230 million going to be divided? For my friend, who represented the wife, there was only one way in which it could be divided—equally. How did he come to that conclusion? Very simply. It was a question of principle. Equitable meant equal. As he told me, there wasn't a judge in the court in which the case would be tried who would not give his client one half.

Needless to say, the husband's attorney had a very different view of the situation and the offer he made was for far less than one half. He felt that $40 million was more than enough. That, of course, got him nowhere, and in an attempt to conclude the matter, he increased his offer. Eventually he increased it to $70 million. It still got him nowhere. Frustrated, the husband's attorney asked my friend, "Does she really need more?" How did my friend respond to the husband's attorney's question? Very simply. He asked, "Does he really need more?"

How did they resolve the matter? They couldn't. They were literally coming from different worlds and, as such, they were not on common ground. The husband's lawyer was talking in terms of need. My friend was talking in terms of principle. Equitable meant equal. As a result, the case eventually went to trial.

The trial judge awarded the wife 45%. My friend decided not to appeal despite the fact that 45% violated his principle. The husband's attorney decided the same thing despite the fact that he felt that 45% was far more than the wife needed.

Why didn't they both appeal? It was really quite simple. The husband's attorney and the wife's attorneys may have lived in different worlds when they were negotiating with one another. But they were suddenly living in the same world once their negotiations broke down. And that world was one of hard reality. Not having a crystal ball, neither attorney knew what the outcome would be if they appealed the court's decision. To be sure, that was true when they went to trial as well. But the court's decision acted as a wake-up call. As the trial judge's decision made clear, once it was out of their hands, how they felt was irrelevant.

I

I do not want to discuss this case any further at this point. But I will in a minute, because it is critical. Instead, I want to address the divorce of a supper-rich couple, which I will define as a couple's whose net worth is in excess of $1 billion dollars. (I could have just as easily referred to a couple whose net worth was in excess of $150 million.) For that purpose, I will turn to Jeff Bezos and his wife, MacKenzie, who had been married for 25 years when they divorced. While there were a number of issues when it came to their settlement (they owned numerous homes all over the world), the principal one concerned their shares of stock in Amazon. To make it very simple, she walked away with approximately 25% of the shares, worth approximately $38.3 billion, and he walked away with the rest.

Let us assume that my friend had represented Mrs. Bezos. Let us further assume that when Mr. Bezos' attorney had offered $38.3 billion and he had rejected it, Mr. Bezos's attorney had asked, does she really need more? Do any of us really believe that my friend would have replied, does he really need more? I don't think that there are any amongst us who believe that he would have. Why not? After all, it is the same principle. That may be true. But it doesn't feel the same here. Why? Because the numbers are very different. And because Mrs. Bezos was never going to keep all of those shares. What was she going to do with them? What she and everyone else in her position did, namely, give them away to various charities. What else could she do with them? What else could Mr. Bezos do with them for that matter. After all, neither of them could take those shares with them.

But it goes well beyond that. The settlement here undermines the rationale that woman's advocates used to justify the idea that our new divorce laws could not be equitable unless they made up to divorcing wives what they had given up in allowing their husbands to go out and advance their own careers while they sacrificed theirs by remaining at home attending to all of their duties as homemakers and the mothers of their children. After all, as any wife and mother will tell you, that kept her busy from morning to night.

Any wife and mother except Mrs. Bezos. She did not clean their home (or any of their many homes). She hired a cleaning service to do that. Did she cook the family's meals? Only if she liked to cook. If she didn't, she hired someone to do the cooking for her. She did not mow her lawn or rake up her leaves. She hired other people to do that as well. In fact, she did not do any of the things that wives normally do. Like most wealthy women, she spent the majority of her time doing what wealthy women do, and that was not freeing up their husband's time so that he could go out and conquer the world. Their husbands could conquer the world without them thank you. Ironically, it was her husband who conquered the world who freed up her time enabling her to do what she so much wanted to do, which was to write two novels. Should he share in any royalties that she earned on that account? After all, fair is fair.

But Mrs. Bezos is not your typical wife you will say, and you would be right. Nevertheless, though the typical wife who employs a divorce lawyer today may not be Mrs. Bezos or even the wife that my friend represented, nor is she the wife who is the prototype of the wife that women's advocates had in mind when they complained about how divorcing wives were being left by our then existing divorce laws. I am talking about the divorcing husbands and wives who turned divorce into the multi-billion dollar a year business that it is today. Those were your better educated upper middle-class husbands and wives. For simplicities sake, I will define them as those whose net worth, exclusive of the equity in their home, is no more than $15 million in today's dollars. I want to define a second group as well. I will refer to them as being very wealthy. I will define them as those whose net worth, again exclusive of the equity in their home, is between $15 million and $30 million in today's dollars.

CHAPTER 6

PRACTICALITY

I have just drawn a line between those divorcing husbands and wives whose net worth, again exclusive of the equity in their home, is not more than $15 million, those where it is between $15 million and $30 million, and those where it is more than $30 million. Those are admittedly arbitrary lines. Thus, when it came to the third, I could have said $40 million or $50 million rather than $30 million. But $30 million will serve my purpose as well. The only purpose of the line at $30 million is to distinguish between those divorces which should be dealt with on the basis of principle—that principle being that *equitable* is equal, and those divorces which should not be. In fact, when it comes to couples whose assets are more than $30 million, they should not be dealt with on the basis of any principle at all. They should be dealt with based on practicality. To put it a little differently, couples in the first and second group would be better served by following a script— basically the one provided by the law. On the other hand, as a general rule couples in the third group would be better served by making it up as they go along. For example, while it is possible that a maintenance payment might be appropriate for the dependent spouse in the first group and even the second group, it is very unlikely that it would be appropriate for the dependent spouse in the third group, whether or not she (or he) was employed.

Why shouldn't couples in the third group also follow a script? After all, isn't what is good for the goose also good for the gander? For two reasons. The first is that our divorce laws were never enacted with them in mind. Second, and even more important, couples in this third group don't have the same problems that couples in the first group do. (That may be true of couples in the second group as well.) They may also have an array of problems and considerations that couples in the first and second groups do not have, which is why our divorce laws are of so little help to them.

I

I am going to address marriages in this first group shortly. Before I do that, however, I want to go back to Mr. and Mrs., Bezos. If they did not follow the script given to them by our divorce laws, how did they come to an agreement? They certainly did not go off to divorce lawyers. By the same token, they did not turn to a divorce mediator either. More important, they did not come to an agreement by turning to our equitable distribution laws as a divorce lawyer would. Nor did they conclude an agreement on the basis of principle—that equitable is equal—as my good friend insisted had to be the case.

Why not? After all, they lived in the state of Washington, a community property state which held that all property acquired during the period of the marriage other than by gift or inheritance had to be divided equally. Because the last thing that Washington's legislature had in mind when they enacted their community property laws was Mr. and Mrs. Bezos.

It must be remembered that before the enactment of our equitable distribution laws, our divorce laws were principally directed at how husbands and wives were going to be able to support themselves and their children following their divorce, not how they were going to deal with their vast savings. They didn't have any. In most instances all that they had was their home, which they lived in, some small savings and their future retirement benefits. As I pointed out in a previous book in this series, the law's "one size fits all" approach when it came to our equitable distribution laws posed enough problems as it was even when it came to your typical husband and wife, which is why it took so long and cost so much for divorcing husbands and wives to conclude an agreement when they turned to the law for help. To suggest that our divorce laws could also shoulder the problems that Mr. and Mrs. Bezos were confronted with, the last of which was how they were each going to be able to support themselves in the future, would be more than ridiculous. It would be to insult our intelligence.

Think about it. Like Bill and Melinda Gates, were they going to establish a charitable trust which they would both manage to handle the billions of dollars that they would be giving to charitable causes? (Mr. and Mrs. Bezos apparently didn't decide to do that.) What was going to happen to Mr. Bezos' $500 million yacht? (What was going to happen to their homes and estates all over the world for that matter?) Most important, how were they going to maintain control of the voting rights when it came to Amazon's stock. And the list went on and on. As I said, to suggest that our equitable distribution laws could address let alone answer any of these questions—that they could be dealt with based on principle—a strict and unbending rule—would be to insult our intelligence.

How then did Mr. and Mrs. Bezos do it? As I am going to characterize it, they just "sat down and worked it out." But what about their *legal rights?* That was one of their legal rights. To be sure, no divorce lawyer with whom they might have consulted would ever have included that in his recitation of their legal rights. On the contrary, the first thing on his list of instructions would be to tell them that he did not want them to discuss any of this with their husband or wife. Why? After all, that was always what they had done in the past—"sat down and worked it out." But that was their marriage, this was their divorce, and for a divorce lawyer all bets were off.

But I am going to go further. I am going to argue that since our equitable distribution laws were not enacted with marriages such as theirs in mind, if husbands and wives in their position turn to the law rather than follow my advice and "sit down and work it out", they will completely lose control of the matter. For example, since Washington, where they live, is a community property state which divides all community property in half, if they turned to the law and applied its inflexible rule. the shares in Amazon and everything else they owned would have been divided strictly based on principle—right down the middle. Put another way, all of the considerations that were important to them would be completely ignored as being irrelevant. To be sure, there may have been good reasons why those states adopted community property laws, just as there were good reasons why so many states changed their divorce laws to equitable distribution laws starting in the early 1960's. But, as I have argued, that does not mean that the reasons behind their enactment are as valid today as they were then.

But it is worse than that, far worse. It is not bad enough that in so many instances our divorce laws incorporate a "one size fits all" approach to the problem, with the result that their application doesn't really fit anyone very well. It is not bad enough that our divorce laws are being applied to a group of divorcing husbands and wives who our state legislatures never had in mind when they enacted those laws. To add insult to injury, the fact that their size and shape have been so influenced by our adversarial legal system and the divorce lawyers who are its agents, by women's advocates who have their own ax to grind, and by our academic legal community whose only concern was to preserve the supremacy of the law in the discussion, has left us with a set of divorce laws that are nothing less than institutional irresponsibility. Nevertheless, as I have argued over and over again in this series of books—borrowing from Wittgenstein's famous saying—the picture that holds us captive is so strong that we are simply unable to see this despite the very heavy price we pay in the process.

CHAPTER 7

THE LIMITATIONS IN THE LAW

The central message in all of the books about divorce in this series is that, rather than view the law as representing a divorcing husband's and wife's *legal rights,* as a divorce lawyer would have it, and turn divorce into a legal tug of war in which the object is simply to get as much as you can and to give as little as you have to, divorcing husbands and wives should be encouraged to view the law as a common *framework* that they can look to in their effort to conclude an agreement, employing it when it helps, ignoring it when it doesn't. Your common sense is enough to tell you that this is the more sensible and responsible way to go about dealing with the problem. Moreover, if they need help, they are far more likely to get it if they turn to divorce mediation and deal with one another with their hands on top of the table rather than turn to divorce lawyers and deal with one another with their hands under the table—or as I have characterized it, if they "sit down and work it out." Nor does a divorce lawyer's objection to this on the ground that divorcing husbands and wives have conflicting interests carry any weight. That characterization is completely gratuitous and self-serving. It would be just as accurate to say that what they have is simply a difference of opinion. But even if they do have what a divorce lawyer refers to as conflicting interests, they also have interests in common, principal of which is not to allow their conflicting interests to get so out of hand as to do irreparable damage to their over-all best interests. It makes no difference that a divorce lawyer would not understand what I am talking about when I refer to their over-all best interests. Their over-all best interests are no less a casualty on that account.

But the point was not to ignore our divorce laws. After all, they are part of the world we live in. It was simply to look to them and to employ them differently—as I put it, not as a weapon in a legal tug of war but as a common *framework* that divorcing husbands and wives could look to in their effort to conclude an agreement. And I was banking on the fact that they now represented such a common *framework*, and that their reach was now far broader, as justification for my faith that our divorce laws could now discharge that responsibility.

Over time, however, I began to have serious doubts about whether our divorce laws really could shoulder the weight that I was placing on them—as I put it, doubts as to whether they really represented a common *framework*. Those doubts only intensified when I came to terms with the reality that the Copernican revolution that I first called for in *Divorce: The Conflict Between Getting It Right and Getting It Done* would never take place. Divorce lawyers would certainly never agree to it. Making the law clearer by making it a common *framework* would put divorce lawyers out of business. Nor would woman's advocates agree to my proposed Copernican revolution in the law. They were so focused on tipping the scales in favor of divorcing wives and so oblivious to the fact that committing their fate to divorce lawyers and an adversarial divorce proceeding was not doing them any favor, that they were literally incapable of seeing where they had left them, which was to be committed to a procedure that would take forever, cost a king's ransom and then, to add insult to injury, get them nowhere.

That only left the academic legal community. And as the members of that community made clear, they would not lift a finger to dislodge the law from its position at the center of a divorcing husband's and wife's world. To do that might threaten our adversarial legal system's most sacred cow, namely, the law's supremacy, and they would never countenance that. (Though I sent copies of the book that I had written that called for a Copernican revolution in the law to 75 of the most prominent family law professors in the United States, I never heard from even one of them.)

Ironically, even the divorce mediation community wouldn't endorse such a suggestion. As I said, the vast majority of divorce mediators today are simply divorce lawyers dressed in sheep's clothing. Thus, they are as bound to viewing our divorce laws as representing a divorcing husband's and wife's sacred *legal rights* as are divorce lawyers. As a result, they would be constitutionally unable to endorse my proposed Copernican revolution in the law. What was I to do?

I found myself confronted with the reality that my Copernican revolution in the law would never take place when I was writing the second book on divorce in this series, *Divorce: Accepting Imperfect Solutions To Imperfect Problems.* Since my entire argument rested on bringing about a Copernican revolution in the law in which a divorcing husband's and wife's attempt to conclude an agreement rather than the law was the center of the universe, I concluded that I was dead in the water. (I eventually solved that problem to my satisfaction and I will get to that in a moment.)

But after I solved that problem, and after I had sent that book to my publisher, I ran into yet another problem. I came to feel that I was asking and expecting too much of the law. Even if my Copernican revolutions could reduce or eliminate many of the hurdles in our divorce laws that divorcing husbands and wives would have to overcome in their effort to conclude an agreement, that would still leave the law with far more weight than it could shoulder.

That is when I came up with the chapter entitled *An Assumption of Risk An Assumption of Responsibility,* which I added as Chapter 16 after the book had already been sent to my publisher. In many ways I considered it to be the most important idea that I had come up with in the more than 30 years that I had been at this, and I commend that chapter to you. In simple terms it argues that our present divorce laws bear more weight than they can realistically carry—that they are not capable of answering all of the questions and solving all of the problems that husbands and wives find themselves faced with when they decide to divorce—and that we ought to shift some of that weight (the risk and responsibility) on to a divorcing husband's and wife's shoulders.

I

In the chapter prior to this one, I divided divorcing husbands and wives into two groups. The only purpose of that division was to distinguish between those divorcing couples who should follow a script, that script being the one provided by the law, and those who should not—as I characterized it, those who should make it up as they went along. In other words, there was nothing sacrosanct about the division. It was simply one of convenience—what seemed to make sense under the circumstances.

Though that division made sense, there was an inherent problem with it. That was the fact that though those who turn to the law for guidance do not generally see this, our divorce laws adopt "a one size fits all" approach to the problem. It is as if the state had a chain of clothing stores that only sold one size, and therefore fit literally none of its customers. To make this point I am going to cite just one example. But I could cite no end of examples.

The example I am going to cite is the provision in New York's equitable distribution laws when it comes to awards of maintenance (spousal support). There are two questions, First, how much should the payments be? Second, how long should it continue? For simplicities sake, I am only going to address the second. The statute in question ties the duration of the payment to the length of the marriage, as follows:

Length of Marriage	Percentage of length of marriage for which maintenance is payable
0 to 15 years	15% to 30%
15 years to 20 years	30% to 40%
More than 20 years	35% to 50%

I am not going to get into whether or not the answer provided by the law was helpful—in the context here, whether looking to the law enabled the couple here to answer their question and conclude an agreement. There is something that you need to know before you answer that question. I know that you won't believe this, but this was only an "advisory" schedule. In other words, in making his decision, the trial judge could employ it or ignore it as he (or she) saw fit.

To be sure, you will complain that I have prejudiced the issue by pulling a once in a million exception in our divorce laws out of a hat. No, I haven't. Though I don't expect you to understand this, what I just told you is the rule whenever our divorce laws provide that the decision (answer) is in the court's "discretion," which is so often the rule. If that is the case, how could turning to the law here have possibly been of any help to the parties. The only ones who benefitted from it were their divorce lawyers, who were looking for as wide a range of answers as they could get.

II

Am I suggesting that this will not be a problem if you turn to a divorce mediator rather than to divorce lawyers? Absolutely not. It will be a problem wherever you turn. But before I get into that, I want to make something clear if I have not already done so. I never suggested that divorce mediation is a modern panacea. As my definition of divorce mediation acknowledges, it is anything but that. Moreover, as the title and theme of the previous book in this series was intended to make clear, we cannot expect perfect solutions to imperfect problems. That being the case, the choice here is between creating an atmosphere that will hopefully encourage a solution to the problem rather than one that we know from experience will have the opposite effect.

My experience certainly confirms that. Having done it both ways, I can tell you that divorce mediation is unquestionably the better choice. (I didn't say the perfect choice. I said the better choice.) But I do not want to make that decision. I want you to make it.

Suppose it is the husband who will be making the maintenance payment and that they go off to divorce lawyers. What will be their attorneys' positions? How could you know that? After all, you didn't go to law school. But you didn't have to. You know that the husband's attorney will pick the shortest period of time and that the wife's attorney will pick the longest. And what will be the atmosphere in the room when they do that? Not very pleasant.

I made this point in Chapter 6 of *A Common Sense, Practical Guide To Divorce,* where I indicated how the positions taken by the parties' respective lawyers will necessarily have the effect of poisoning the well. How could they do anything but that? After all, their discussions were very formal, calculated and impersonal. It was all simply dollars and cents.

Just the opposite will be the case if they turn to a divorce mediator. To put it more accurately, the divorce mediator they work with will do everything that he (or she) can to create the exact opposite atmosphere. To be sure, despite his effort, he may not succeed in doing that. But that is what he will try to do

In that regard, the first thing that he will do is get to know the two of them. He will refer to that as learning his running room—what will work and what won't work; what he can get away with and what he can't get away with. Yes, they are divorcing, which means that they see things differently. But that doesn't mean that there is no commonality left in their relationship. If they have children, there usually is. And to the extent that there still is such commonality, the mediator they are working with will want to take advantage of it. To be sure, there may be little if any commonality left in their relationship, and if that is the case, he will have to live with that. But husbands and wives do not necessarily divorce because they are completely at odds with one another—that they have absolutely nothing in common. They do so because they are unable to continue to live with one another. Since most divorces are initiated by just one of them, only one of them may feel that way. The point is that while that residual commonality may not have any effect on their ability to conclude an agreement, it may, which is why the mediator they employ will want to use it to his advantage if he can.

III

Unfortunately, it would take us to far afield for me to go into all of the ways in which a mediator will attempt to bring the two of them to an agreement. Nevertheless, so that you will have a better sense of this, I will mention a few.

If a divorce lawyer is unable to conclude an agreement for his client, it is because he is unable to get it right—at least as he sees it. What is his solution? To go back and try harder. If a husband and wife are unable to conclude an agreement in mediation, it is because they are stuck. That being the case, the mediator's effort will not be directed at getting it right. He knows that that is only a divorce lawyer's conceit. He will direct his efforts at getting them unstuck.

How can he do that? Sometimes by changing the subject. Consider the duration of the maintenance payment. If the parties have not been married more than 15 years, the payment is between 15% and 30% of the length of the marriage. But the parties are stuck. The wife believes it should be 30% of the length of the marriage. The husband believes that it should be 15 %. How can the mediator change the subject? By suggesting that the payment will be made for 30% of the length of the marriage but that, if the wife establishes her residence with someone with whom she is conducting a romantic relationship in that time, the payments will be reduced by one-half. Or, if the wife's income from employment increases within that time, the amount of the payment will decrease by 50% of the increase in her income from employment. But that is not what a judge would direct if the matter went to court. So what? That is only because the statute did not give the judge the power to do that. But there is no law that says that the two them cannot include a provision to that effect in their agreement.

Let me give one more example. Very often, particularly where there are infant children, the parties will provide that the one with whom the children will maintain their primary residence (usually the wife) will have the right to continue to live in their home until the youngest child graduates from high school. That is all well and good. But it raises a whole host of questions. If the wife forms a new romantic relationship, will she have the right to permit that person to move into the home? What if she remarries. The list is almost endless.

Divorce lawyers tend to ignore them. And there is good reason to. To address them is literally to open a can of worms, and it is going to be hard enough for them to conclude an agreement as it is without making it harder.

Be that as it may, the divorce mediator they work with will not do that—at least he won't if he follows the roadmap outlined in in this series of books. As I have mentioned, there is a Workbook that accompanies this series of books that contains a list of questions that will be addressed in the course of the mediation. There are 34 questions in the section of that Workbook addressed to the parties' home that have to be answered in their agreement. As a result, there is no chance that the issue I have just raised, and 33 others, will not be addressed.

Won't that make it harder. Yes, but unlike a divorce lawyer, a divorce mediator (at least one who follows the roadmap outlined in this series of books) will have the benefit of that Workbook to make it a little easier for him and he will use it to his advantage.

I said that there are 34 questions in the section of the Workbook devoted to their home. But, with the exception of the answers to the first 7 questions, the Workbook will suggest the answers to all of the rest. (For example, when it comes to the question of the cost of future repairs to the home, while the couple will answer the more basic ones, such as who will be responsible for the cost of any repair up to a certain amount, the Workbook will suggests the answer when it comes to repairs in excess of that amount.) Moreover, since the balance of the questions are more ministerial, and since the couple know that the answers were not arrived at with them in mind, they will be more pre-disposed to accept them. (Strike one up for divorce mediation.)

IV

Will adopting the approach I have suggested enable the two of them to get it right, whatever that means? I never said that. That was not the mediator's objective. It enabled them to get "unstuck"—in the terms that I have expressed it, to get it done—and that was sufficient. Why not both? Because, while it is possible to define what it means to get it done, it is not possible to define what it means to get it right, which is why no two divorce lawyers will ever agree when it comes to that. Again, we are talking about the application of legal rules, which vary from state to state, not the rules of mathematics, which are universal.

There is one last point that I want to make in this regard. The setting provided in divorce mediation makes it much easier for divorcing husbands and wives to deal with the conflict between getting it right and getting it done. It isn't that they don't want to get it right, whatever that means. It is that, unlike what happens when divorcing husbands and wives turn to divorce lawyers, getting it right doesn't become a quasi-religious goal that blocks out all reality. What reality am I talking about? The reality that is the theme of all three of the books about divorce in this series, namely, that we cannot expect perfect solutions to imperfect problems. Again, to put it in Wittgenstein's terms, that is the picture that holds us captive that we must free ourselves from. That is why, when I talk about getting it right, I always add, "whatever that means."

V

I want to close by saying one last thing about the setting in which an adversarial divorce proceeding and a divorce mediation each takes place. Again, I am not suggesting that they are black and white—that one has only bad features and the other only good ones. But I am insisting that there is a vast difference when it comes to the settings in which they take place, and that difference can have a significant effect on the success of the undertaking.

With that in mind I am going to contrast the two by saying that one is informal and the other formal; that one is personal and the other impersonal; that one inevitably highlights what are still areas of commonality in your relationship and the other the areas of conflict. The fact that a divorce lawyer only meets with one of you privately, while a divorce mediator only meets with the two of you together, tends to account for that. The fact that the discussions are between your two attorneys in one case, while the discussions are between the two of you in the other, also tends to account for that. As is often said, context is everything.

But there is something else that accounts for this as well. A divorce mediator will very consciously attempt to make it personal. He (or she) will do that at the very first meeting that he has with the two of them. Not personal in the hugs and kisses sense. (A divorce mediator always wants it to be professional.) More in "a friend of the family" sense.

What the two of them are embarking upon is going to be difficult. But a divorce mediator does not want it to be any more difficult than it has to be. And one of the things that may make it a little easier for the two of them is if they feel that they are working with someone—a friend of the family if you wish—who is on their side, and who they can look to for help. Compromises will have to be made. As I said, one cannot expect perfect solutions to imperfect problems. But hopefully the mediator that the two of them are working with, and the trust that they come to have in him (or her), will make it a little easier for them to do that.

That is no mean achievement. That is why, when it comes to selecting a divorce mediator, I have emphasized the importance of selecting someone who views the undertaking from the perspective outlined in this series of books, and who is smart and insightful, rather than someone who is anything but that—someone who I characterized as just flying by the seat of his pants.

CHAPTER 8

REDEFINING THE TERMS OF THE DEBATE

This book has been entitled *Divorce: Redefining the Terms of the Debate*. Admittedly, I did not think in those terms when I first sat down and started writing books about divorce and divorce mediation. I didn't even think in those terms when I started to write the first book about divorce in this series, *A Common Sense, Practical Guide To Divorce*. The idea of redefining the terms of the debate only came to me when I sat down to write the second book on divorce in this series and, as I said, I ran into rather serious problems. To be sure, as is always the case, even though I didn't know how, I felt that I would somehow solve them, which I did. The brick wall that I had run into just forced me to think deeper in order to do that.

That is when I came up with what became the central theme of the books on divorce in this series, namely, that one cannot expect perfect solutions to imperfect problems. A perfect solution would be that turning to our divorce laws would answer all of a divorcing couple's questions and solve all of their problems.

Not as our divorce laws are now. That is the last thing they would do. In their present form, they will actually create more problems than they will solve. That is why I proposed a Copernican revolution in the law. But as I was forced to admit, that revolution would never take place. It was tantamount to asking a very conservative Republican who championed a fetus' right to life to accept a woman's right to terminate that potential life by having an abortion. And visa-versa. That was never going to happen. The contending factions would rather take to the street than do that. That being the case, I had to accept the reality that those who were held captive by a picture of divorce that sanctified our divorce laws as representing the parties' *legal rights*, and placed them at the center of our legal universe, would never accept my Copernican revolution in the law.

What then was the answer? That is when the idea of redefining the terms of the debate came into the conversation. Since there would be no Copernican revolution in the law, divorce lawyers would continue to view and employ our divorce laws as they always had, namely, as weapons in a legal tug of war. What then were divorce mediators who rejected a divorce lawyer's irresponsible picture of the world of divorce, and its damaging consequences, going to do? It was very simple. Unless our divorce laws provided divorcing husbands and wives with clear answers to their questions and solutions to their problems, divorce mediators who have, in my terms, redefined the terms of the debate, would simply ignore our divorce laws. After all, except in those few instances where their application is mandatory, such as when it comes to child support, one of a divorcing husband's and wife's legal rights is to ignore our divorce laws and to make it up as they go along—as I put it, to "sit down and work it out."

I

Will turning to divorce mediation and defining the debate in the terms that I have proposed answer all of a divorcing couple's questions and solve all of their problems? Of course not. As I have repeatedly said, we do not live in a transcendental world of possible perfection as our Western philosophical and religious traditions would have us believe. Rather, we live in a very imperfect world, one of inevitable constraint and human limitation, and in such a world, compromises will necessarily have to be made.

But as I realized after I had finished the previous book on divorce in this series, it goes beyond that. As I pointed out in Chapter 16 of that previous book, the world that we live in today is very different than it was even 75 years ago, before the enactment of our equitable distribution laws. Unlike their husbands, most women then did not go to college, let alone graduate school. Unlike their husbands, they were not bread winners. They were home makers. Just as important, nearly one-half of all marriages in the United States did not end in divorce. Thus, though it would quickly change, when our equitable distribution statutes were originally enacted, they were a fairly accurate picture of the world of marriage and divorce.

But as I realized when I was finishing that second book, what was true 75 years ago was not true today. The world had dramatically changed in that time. Thus, though it may not have been appropriate to think in terms of an assumption of risk and an assumption of responsibility when those equitable distribution statutes were enacted, it most certainly was now.

Would any of us deny that a couple who marries today assumes the risk that their marriage may end in divorce? Would any of us today deny that a woman who marries today who has a college (and perhaps even a graduate school) degree, and is gainfully employed, like her husband, assumes a financial responsibility in the event that their marriage ends in divorce. And should that responsibility be any less because our equitable distribution statutes do not accurately reflect how our world has changed in that time? It is, or at least should be, a rhetorical question.

II

That is my answer to the problem. (I said answer, not solution.) Just as those who marry today necessarily assume a risk, namely, that instead of going the distance, their marriage may end in divorce, they also assume a responsibility in the event that is the case. And that is as true of a wife as it is of her husband. To be sure, the wives that I am talking about are not the same wives as those who got divorced 75 years ago, who in most cases had little if any ability to bear any portion of that responsibility.

They are those wives who get divorced today, and since the women I am talking about have the same opportunity as their husbands, they have an obligation to conduct their lives following their marriage in such a way as to be able to assume some of that responsibility if their marriage ends in divorce.

I don't want to be misunderstood here. I am not suggesting that wives should have a responsibility and that their husbands should not. I am just saying that, whereas in the past we were only talking about a husband's responsibility in the event that their marriage ended in divorce, today we should be talking about both of their responsibilities should that happen.

In retrospect, I think that my introduction of the idea of risk and responsibility, together with my suggestion that we should re-characterize the undertaking as the parties "sitting down and working it out", were perhaps the two most important contributions that I have made to the discussion. These ideas are not going to have any significant impact on lower class or even middle-class families. But they are not generally the ones who look to the law or retain divorce lawyers when they divorce. They get the necessary forms that they need from the court and do this pretty much on their own. Nor is it going to have any significant impact on the super-rich, like Mr. and Mrs. Bezos. They are not going to turn to divorce lawyers or the law. Our equitable distribution statutes do not apply to them either. We are talking about upper-middle class or very wealthy husbands and wives—the husbands and wives who now still turn to divorce lawyers and our divorce laws, and who have made divorce the multi-billion dollar a year industry that it presently is.

But I think that the idea of risk and responsibility, combined with my re-characterization of the undertaking, were perhaps the most important contributions that I made to the discussion for another, even more important reason. They can only be incorporated into the discussion if a divorcing husband and wife turn to divorce mediation and, even then, not to just any divorce mediator.

Why will they not be able to turn to a divorce lawyer? Because no divorce lawyer will accept the conditions that are necessary to follow the roadmap outlined in this series of books. He (or she) will certainly not conduct his practice as if there has been a Copernican revolution in the law which had the effect of providing divorcing husbands and wives with clear answers to their questions and solutions to their problems. It would reduce adversarial divorce proceedings to a "once was" And how could a divorce lawyer continue to play his game if he recommended that the two of them should "sit down and work it out." Divorce would no longer be the multi-billion dollar a year industry that it is now. It might not be an industry at all.

But those two contributions are going to have another important effect. They are going to significantly improve the quality of divorce mediation. They are going to separate the wheat from the chaff. I have made no pretense of the fact that, if "sitting down and working it out" as Mr. and Mrs. Bezos did won't do, I am very much in favor of a husband and wife turning to a divorce mediator rather than to divorce lawyers. But I have also made it clear that I am not happy with most of those who are currently practicing divorce mediation and, as I put it, the roadmap that they are following. (I will get into that a little later when I return to how you should go about selecting a divorce mediator.) Hopefully, this series of books will have two effects. First, to cause those who do not belong acting as divorce mediators to leave the business before they are put out of business. Second, to provide those who do belong in the field with a roadmap that will enable them to become better divorce mediators.

CHAPTER 9

FOLLOWING THE RIGHT ROADMAP

Unless you are a member of the academic legal community who teaches family law, if you are reading any of the books in this series about divorce, it is because you are faced with the prospect of divorce in your own marriage and you are trying to decide how to proceed. I am also assuming that, in your case, you are going to need help and that the only question is where you will turn to get it. Will it be to a divorce lawyer (or collaborative family lawyer) or will it be to a divorce mediator. If it is to a divorce mediator, will it be to a mediator who follows the script (roadmap) that I have laid out in this series of books on divorce or will it be to one who, as I have characterized him or her, is simply a divorce lawyer dressed in sheep's clothing?

This may surprise you, but I am not going to express an opinion here. To be sure, you know how I think. I have told you that. But that is as far as I am going to go. Let me explain.

I live by an expression. I am not responsible for the world. I didn't create the world. I am only responsible for myself. Thus, so long as I have discharged that obligation in an appropriate manner, the problem is no longer mine. I like to think that I have done that here. If that is the case, it would be inappropriate for me to intrude further. This is your life not mine.

I

Let me explain this a little better. Through the strangest of circumstances (which I won't go into) I found myself representing divorcing husbands and wives in traditional adversarial divorce proceedings and in time I had attained some prominence in the field, having been admitted as a Fellow in the American Academy of Matrimonial Lawyers. Though I had some misgivings about what I was doing (really with the attorneys and judges that I had to deal with), I was able to manage them.

That all changed with the enactment of New York's equitable distribution laws and the introduction of divorce mediation. Instinctively, I knew that divorce mediation was the way I wanted to go and within a very short time I stopped practicing as a divorce lawyer and only accepted husbands and wives who wanted to mediate their divorce. I should add that though I had attended the first nationwide conference devoted to the practice of divorce mediation, I had absolutely no training as a divorce mediator, not even an hour's worth. Nevertheless, I had already prepared a workbook, similar to the one in this series, that I gave to husbands and wives who retained my services.

And within a short time, I also began to write books on the subject. Initially I viewed my first two books as my "practice books." That all changed with my third book, *Divorce Mediation: A Practice in Search of a Theory,* which I began thinking about in the early 1990's and published in 1997. By then I had come to realize that most divorce mediators were simply divorce lawyers dressed in sheep's clothing, by which I meant that they basically followed the same roadmap as a divorce lawyer did, one which put the law at the center of their universe. As I said in that book, though they viewed divorce mediation to be a total rejection of adversarial divorce proceedings, since they had unwittingly given the very same answers as divorce lawyers did to the four basic questions that anyone working with divorcing husbands and wives had to ask and answer, they could not be anything but that? Needless to say, though I had been the President of the New York State Council on Divorce Mediation, that suggestion did not ingratiate me with the divorce mediation community any more than it did with the matrimonial bar. In short, within no time I was practicing divorce mediation unlike anyone else in the field. I was literally a minority of one.

The point is that you cannot expect every divorce mediator you meet with to view your problem or our divorce laws as I have presented them, or follow the roadmap that I have recommended. Unless he (or she) has read these companion books, he will not even know what you are talking about. Rather, just like a divorce lawyer, he will view our divorce laws as representing your *legal rights* and will refer to them as such during the course of the mediation. He (or she) will certainly not conduct a divorce mediation as if a Copernican revolution in our divorce laws has taken place, and if you referred to any such revolution, he would not know what you were talking about. The same would be true when it came to the idea of an assumption of risk and an assumption of responsibility that I have introduced into the conversation. If you referred to them, it would be as if you were speaking a foreign language.

That is fine. Maybe the roadmap that he is following is the better one. Again, that is for you to decide. But you should know what roadmap he is following. You can't assume that they are all the same. As I hope you have learned from reading the books on divorce in this series, they are anything but that.

How can you find out the answer to that question? Ask him to give you a copy of the book that sets forth the roadmap that he is following. I didn't say ask him to give you a copy of the book he has written on the subject. I don't expect every divorce mediator you meet with to have written a book. Nor is it necessary. For example, if he says that he has read and follows the books that I have written, or if he refers to a book that someone else has written that he says he follows, if you read it, you will now be an educated consumer. But you must satisfy yourself that you know where he is taking you, the roadmap that he will be following to get there, and whether you feel comfortable with it. And if he cannot give you the name of the book that he follows, that means that he is flying blind or, as we say, by the seat of his pants. It is that simple.

If you have read *The Book About Marriage: Entering It, Sustaining It, Ending It,* you know that the reason I feel that most mental health professionals are of so little help to couples who come to them with the problems that they are having in their marriage, is that they are following the wrong roadmap. And what is true when it comes to mental health professionals is true of divorce mediators and divorce lawyers as well.

Why do divorce lawyers make such a mess of it. Because they are following the wrong roadmap. The same is true of a divorce mediator. If he (or she) does not follow the right roadmap, he has far less chance of helping a husband and wife answer the questions and solve the problems that they are faced with as a result of their decision to divorce, thereby enabling them to conclude an agreement. To be sure, the fact that he is following the right roadmap is no guarantee that he will succeed. But if he does follow the right roadmap, and if he (or she) is the right person, he stands a far better chance. Who is the right person? I will get into that in a moment.

II

I have very purposely not gotten into how you should select a divorce lawyer if you decide to turn to an adversarial divorce proceeding, though I somewhat did that in the first book on divorce in this series. But that was not really to help you decide on the divorce lawyer you would employ if you went down that road. It was to help you cut through all of the window dressing that he (or she) used to distract you, thereby enabling you to get a better look at what you will be getting yourself into if you follow the roadmap that he is recommending.

Am I saying that, since all divorce lawyers follow the same roadmap, they are all the same? Absolutely not. They are anything but that. In fact, there was one who I knew quite well, and with whom I had a few matters over the years, who was anything but that, and if I could have been guaranteed that he would be my opposing counsel in every one of my cases, I would never have had to go into divorce mediation. Was that because he was not a divorce lawyer in the true sense of that term? You would have fooled the American Academy of Matrimonial Lawyers. He was one of its past Presidents. It was because of the person who he was. Unfortunately, that was not the case with most of the divorce lawyers that I found myself dealing with.

In most instances, I was dealing with very different people, and this was true even when it came to Fellows of the American Academy of Matrimonial Lawyers. They were constitutionally different. As we say, they were difficult people. Unfortunately, all too often they were the ones that your Greek chorus would have recommended to you. As they would tell you, you need to get a "tough" lawyer. Unfortunately, what you don't know is that if you follow their counsel, the only thanks that you will get is to end up with a tough divorce.

But there was more to it than that. After all, the attorney in question will be functioning in an adversarial legal system where the goal is to get as much as you can and to give as little as you have to. To add to the problem, like my friend who had been the President of his state's bar association, they will be held captive by a picture that places the law at the center of their universe, thereby making the issue in question a matter of principle. There will also be divorce lawyers who are aggressive by nature, and the setting in which they conduct their business will encourage them to give free reign to their aggression. Finally, and this was all too often the case with the divorce lawyers I had to deal with, there will be their inflated egos. In short, it was a terrible mix, which was why it was so painful, took so long, and cost so much.

CHAPTER 10

BUILDING IN AN ASSESSMENT

Before I turn to how to go about selecting a divorce mediator, I want to address one last issue. Again, it is a carry-over from *The Book About Marriage*.

I took strong issue in that book with how mental health professionals all too often just sat there listening to the problems that husbands and wives came to them with, without making any real progress, until one or both of them became so tired and frustrated that they just got up and left. I felt that the mental health professionals in question owed more to them than that. What he (or she) owed to them was his opinion as to whether or not he thought that they were making any progress and, if not, whether there was any point in their continuing to meet with him. I referred to that as an "assessment."

But there was more to the assessment than that. If the mental health professional in question felt that it made sense for them to continue to meet with him, he was also obligated to give them a time frame—three months, six months or whatever—in which they would see that progress and, if there was not any in that time, to terminate his participation in the undertaking.

The same should be true here. If you turn to a divorce mediator, you do not expect that it will take the two of you one year or more to conclude an agreement. Perhaps 3 or 4 months, but not one year or more. By the same token, if you turn to divorce lawyers, you do not expect that it will take the two of you between 2 and 3 years to conclude an agreement. Maybe between 7 or 8 months, but not between 2 and 3 years.

That is where the assessment comes in. Before you employ the divorce mediator you are considering or retain the divorce lawyer you are considering, you want him (or her) to tell you two things. First, how long does he believe it will take for the two of you to conclude an agreement. Second to agree that, if you have not been able to conclude an agreement in that time, he will recommend that you go down the other road—in the case of a divorce lawyer, recommend that you turn to a divorce mediator; in the case of a divorce mediator, recommend that you turn to divorce lawyers. I will tell you in advance that no divorce lawyer will be willing to do that. I will also tell you in advance that any divorce mediator who follows the roadmap laid out in these companion books will be willing to do that.

I

There is one last thing that I wish to borrow from *The Book About Marriage.* I already mentioned this in passing in one of the previous books in this series. I now want to introduce it more formally.

In an important sense you are flying blind. You do not know what your chances are if you go down one of those roads rather than the other. The only thing that you know is that it will be far more painful, take a great deal longer, and cost significantly more if you go down a divorce lawyer's road than it will if you go down a divorce mediator's road. In fact, the retainer (down payment) that each of you will be required to ante up if you go down the road that a divorce lawyer will recommend will be far more for each of you than the total fee that both of you will pay if you go down the road that a divorce mediator will recommend. And that is just the retainer. What do you have to lose? The point is that if you follow my recommendation, you are not really deciding. You are just testing out. Let me explain.

As I said, I do not think that any divorce lawyer will be willing to tell you how long it will take, let alone agree that if he has not been able conclude an agreement for you in that time, you should turn to a divorce mediator. But a divorce mediator will be willing to answer that question and agree to that condition. Just ask him.

Suppose that a divorce mediator tells you that it will take 3 to 4 months. Suppose that a divorce lawyer tells you that it will take between 12 months and 18 months, or suppose that he will not give you any time frame at all. What do you have to lose if you employ the divorce mediator? Just 3 or 4 months. If he has not helped you conclude an agreement in that time, you can always turn to divorce lawyers. But suppose a divorce lawyer has told you that it will take between 12 months and 18 months. Then you have to assume that you will have to wait a lot longer to find out whether or not he will succeed. If he has been unwilling to give you any answer (which will be the case), you may have to wait forever.

If it is a gamble either way, what are the odds. In one case 3 or 4 months. In the other 12 to 18 months (assuming you are given any odds at all). It is really that simple. Which is the better bet. Remember, it is not just the time. It is also the cost. If you retain divorce lawyers, the retainer that each of you will be asked to put down will be more than the total cost for both of you if you employ a divorce mediator. And that is just the retainer. The total cost will be three to five times the amount of your retainer. As they say, it is a no-brainer.

I have to add one thing, I said that a divorce lawyer will never be willing to answer your question. How can he avoid doing that? By changing the subject in one of two ways. First, by telling you that it all depends upon how reasonable or unreasonable your husband or wife and their respective lawyers will be—the implication being that it will not be his fault if the two of you are not able to conclude an agreement. Second, by telling you that the divorce mediator you employ will not be interested in getting it right—securing your legal rights. He will only be interested in getting it done. To be sure, your divorce lawyer will not be willing to tell you what your legal rights are, let alone that he will be able to secure them. But he can't possibly know whether the agreement he will conclude for you will be better or worse than the one you will conclude if you employ a divorce mediator. As he has told you, that depends on how reasonable or unreasonable his opposing counsel is, and he doesn't know that. Again, like so much of what a divorce lawyer will tell you, it will just be so much talk—meaningless window dressing.

CHAPTER 11

SELECTING A DIVORCE MEDIATOR

In a previous book in this series, I discussed meeting with both a divorce lawyer and a divorce mediator and, when it came to a divorce mediator, the questions you should ask him (or her). I did the same when it came to a divorce lawyer, but for a different reason. The questions in each case were designed to give you a better sense of the difference between going down one of those roads (as I have put it, following one of those roadmaps) rather than the other.

The question here is a little different. You have decided which of those two roads you want to go down. The question now is who you are going to select as your guide. You will excuse me if I do not get into who you should choose if you turn to an adversarial divorce proceeding, which is what you will be doing if you turn to a divorce lawyer (and, as far as I am concerned, to a collaborative family lawyer as well). So, if you have decided to go down that other road, I will just say that you would be better off selecting a collaborative family lawyer and, in either case, someone who is a Fellow of the American Academy of Matrimonial Lawyers. You at least know that he or she is a very qualified divorce lawyer.

I

Before I get into the question of how you should go about selecting a divorce mediator, I want to put something to rest. There is no question that I think that you would be making a mistake if you turned to divorce lawyers and that, regardless of their good intensions, those who suggest that you should are doing you a great disservice. An adversarial divorce proceeding is nothing less than a form of institutional irresponsibility. And all of the fancy window dressing that divorce lawyers employ to sell their wares does not change that.

But I do not want to be misunderstood here. As I have consistently acknowledged, I do not believe that there is anything wonderful about divorce mediation, and I have a big problem with divorce mediators whose web page romanticizes it by featuring a picture of a smiling husband and wife and their children. You should immediately cross them off your list of possible candidates. More to the point, I made that as clear as I could from the very beginning. Thus, on the very first page of Chapter 1 of *Divorce Mediation: A Practice in Search of a Theory,* I defined divorce mediation as follows:

> It is an imperfect procedure
> That employs an imperfect third person
> To help two imperfect people
> Conclude an imperfect agreement
> In an imperfect world

And I have never changed that opinion. It is simply the best of the possible choices, none of which is perfect. Unfortunately, divorce mediators, and the Academy of Professional Family Mediators (APFM) which is their spokesperson, are not content to leave it at that. Though they do not exactly suggest that divorce mediation is the next best thing since ice tea, they most certainly do suggest that mediation can be used to solve no end of the problems that society is faced with. My point is very simple. With the exception of the death of a child or someone very close, husbands and wives who decide to divorce are faced with the most difficult problem they will ever encounter in their lives, and those who have stepped forward to offer assistance to them at this critical time are anything but of one mind when it comes to what is the best way to help them. The only thing that we know is that, whether we are divorce mediators, divorce lawyers, collaborative family lawyer or whatever, we could do it better. That being the case, before APFM and the divorce mediation community goes out to save the world, it would be better if they cleaned up their own house. And as someone who has labored in this undertaking for over 50 years, I can tell you that the first order of business is to raise the standards and improve the quality of those who practice divorce mediation. I appreciate the fact that APFM will be offened by this suggestion. But that does not render my judgment any less valid.

II

With that I will now turn to the question of how you should go about selecting a divorce mediator.

I went into this somewhat in Chapter 24 of a previous book in this series, *A Common Sense, Practical Guide To Divorce*. But I would like to approach it here from a slightly different angle.

There is nothing that will tell you whether the divorce mediator you are meeting with is really qualified and you would be making a big mistake if you put any significance in what he (or she) will tell you or show you to persuade you that he is. Dismiss out of hand the certificate on the wall of his office which attests to the fact that he has completed a 40 hour training course in divorce mediation. No one who is really qualified to be a divorce mediator would put that certificate on his (or her) wall. It is just so much meaningless window dressing.

It is very different with a divorce lawyer. If he (or she) has a certificate on his wall attesting to the fact that he is a Fellow of the American Academy of Matrimonial lawyers, you know that he is a qualified divorce lawyer. There is no such certificate in the field of divorce mediation.

But suppose you follow my advice and never hire anyone who is not a lawyer. Shouldn't he or she also be a Fellow of the American Academy of

Matrimonial Lawyers (AAML)? No. He couldn't be. Like me, he would have to have been a divorce lawyer before he became a divorce mediator, and there is almost no practicing divorce mediator other than myself who was. AAML only accepts divorce lawyers.

The point is that you should never assume that the person you are meeting with is qualified to be a divorce mediator. It is for him (or her) to convince you that he is. How could he do that? The answer was staring me right in the face and I didn't see it.

If you have read *The Book About Marriage: Entering it, Sustaining It. Ending It,* you know that I argue that the reason most metal health professionals are of so little help to husbands and wives who come to them is that they are following the wrong roadmap. The point is that, regardless of the approach they take, they have to have a roadmap. If the divorce mediator you meet with has read the books on divorce in this series, you know that he (or she) has a roadmap and what it prescribes. If he hasn't read them, unless he has another roadmap, he is flying blind— as we say, by the seat of his pants. Obviously, you do not want to employ someone who is flying by the seat of his pants.

I don't think that this will happen, but suppose he tells you that he is following a roadmap, but it is a different one than the one that I am prescribing. Fine. Ask him to give you the name of the book that prescribes it and read it for yourself. If you feel that it is better than the roadmap that I have described in this series of books, employ him (or her). It is that simple.

III

Let us assume that you are meeting with two different divorce mediators both of whom follow the same roadmap. How do you decide between them? Obviously, whom you feel more comfortable with will be an important factor. But I want to add a second consideration. All things being equal, employ the one who you think is smarter.

Before I get into that, I want to tell you that I think that this is one of the most important things that I will tell you. When I am talking about smart, I am not talking about someone's I.Q., though very smart people usually have higher I.Q.s. In fact, I am not talking about anything that you can test for. I am talking about things that you feel someone has, like insight and understanding. Very smart people usually have more of that as well. And it is the most important thing that they can give to you. It may be hard to see that if you view the undertaking to be one of negotiating an equitable distribution case. But you will hopefully sense it if you view the undertaking as I have portrayed it, namely, to help the two of you to "sit down and work it out." That is why I did not say that the divorce mediator you choose to work with has to have the same credentials that you would look for if he was a divorce lawyer— that he be a Fellow of the American Academy of Matrimonial Lawyers. He is not functioning as a divorce lawyer. I only said that he should be a lawyer—someone who knows our divorce laws. While I do not think that they are sacred, as a divorce lawyer does, I never suggested that they are not important, by which I mean useful. And if they can be, you want someone who knows something about them. Moreover, since this is all going to end by the two you entering into a binding legal agreement, you want him (or her) to know something about preparing that as well. And as any qualified lawyer will tell you, drafting a legal document is one of the hardest things that he is ever required to do.

But there is another reason why a divorce mediator does not need the same credentials as a divorce lawyer. There may be some methodology involved in "negotiating an equitable distribution case" or "mediating a divorce", though I think that those who suggest that are making too much of this. But there is no methodology involved in "sitting down and working it out." On the contrary, it is to abandon all such supposed methodologies and substitute something more valuable and important. Where will you find that? Hopefully in the very smart person who you select to help you and whose insight and understanding you have come to respect and trust. Before I retired, I had the privilege of working with three women who had those qualifications. None of them was a Fellow of The American Academy of Matrimonial Lawyers. But they were every bit as smart as anyone I knew in The American Academy of Matrimonial Lawyers.

That still leaves you with a question. How do you determine whether the person you are meeting with is smart? It is really quite simple. Ask him (or her) to explain the message in this series of books on divorce. Someone who can do that is smart in my sense of that term. Someone who can't isn't. All things being equal, select the divorce mediator who is best able to do that. It will not be so much what he (or she) says. It will be how he conveys it to you. Does he (or she) make you feel that you are in good hands. Remember, he is trying to help the two of you to "sit down and work it out." If he does, you are in good hands.

IV

As I have already said, I do not believe that there are very many practicing divorce mediators today who have those necessary qualifications. Nor are there very many who would describe what they do in the terms that I have expressed it.

I appreciate the fact that the Academy of Professional Family Mediators (APFM) will take strong exception to this, as they will to literally everything that I have said in this series of books. That is because APFM is more of a club than a professional association, and their rank and file (which is open to anyone) is more interested in presenting themselves as qualified practitioners than they are in assuring that those who join their ranks pass that test.

PART II

REDEFINING THE TERMS OF THE DEBATE

CHAPTER 12

SITTING DOWN AND WORKING IT OUT

I have characterized this last book on divorce in this series as redefining the terms of the debate.

Up until this point, the terms of the debate have been defined by no end of groups. There are divorce lawyers. There are collaborative family lawyers. There are divorce mediators who are really divorce lawyers dressed in sheep's clothing. There are women's advocates who view the object of the undertaking to be to compensate divorcing wives for what they lost in marrying and becoming homemakers and mothers to their children. And, of course, there is the academic legal community. The list is almost endless.

To make matters worse, there are also no end of approaches to the problem. There are those who believe that equitable means equal—at least if they represent wives who are in the one-down position. There are others who take exception to the suggestion that equitable is equal —at least if they represent husbands who are in the one-up position. There are those, like Professors Mnookin and Kornhauser, who don't seem to have any opinion except that our divorce laws, like the sun, should be at the center of a divorcing husband's and wife's universe.

And now there is me, who believes that in most cases what divorcing husbands and wives have been left with is nothing less than institutional irresponsibility and that it is time to stop that. You want to continue to play your fun and games with divorcing husbands' and wives' lives. Fine, do that. I want to offer divorcing husbands and wives who do not want to play that game a choice by redefining the terms of the debate. That is to offer them the opportunity, as I have characterized it, to "sit down and work it out." For simplicity's sake, it will still be referred to as divorce mediation. However, in practice, it will be characterized as "sitting down and working it out."

Is it a radically new approach? No. As I said, there isn't a radical bone in my body. It really isn't even revolutionary. How could it be if it is what husbands and wives did in their marriage when they were confronted with a question or had a problem. After all, did they call in lawyers? Of course not. They "sat down and worked it out."

Does sitting down and working it out mean that they will no longer turn to the law? Again, I never said that. In some instances, they have no choice. Child support payments, for instance, which are mandatory, are defined by the law. But in the vast majority of instances the law doesn't tell divorcing husbands and wives what to do. It says "do what you want." If that is the case, they will look to the law when it helps and ignore it when it doesn't. One thing they won't do is make a game out of it. Another thing they won't do is judge the agreement they conclude by a legal yardstick. As I said in the first book on divorce in this series, if they didn't do that in their marriage, why would they do that in their divorce? But what about their legal rights. As I said, they are exercising one of their legal rights when they do that.

I

This is how I have redefined the terms of the debate. I have proposed a completely new approach to the problems that husbands and wives find themselves faced with when they decide to divorce. As I have put it, they should "sit down and work it out."

But I do not want to leave it at that. It doesn't tell divorcing husbands and wives where to start. I therefore want to suggest a framework that they might start with. But before I do that, I want to make something clear. I will not be speaking based on my experience as a divorce lawyer. I will not be speaking based on my experience as a divorce mediator. I won't be speaking based on any experience. Like almost everything else in this series of books, it is just something that I thought out and came up with over time. So how are you to judge what I am going to suggest? In the same way that you judged everything that I have said up to this point? Does it make sense? Does it help? Has anyone else suggested another framework that makes more sense and helps more? If they have, you should ignore what I am going to say and listen to them.

If you have read the other books on divorce in this series, you know that one of my complaints when it comes to our current divorce laws is that, time and time again, they employ a "one size fits all approach" to the problem. One example that I gave was the law's approach to the payment that a husband was to make to his wife in the event of her remarriage. It was to terminate whether they had been married for only five years or whether they had been married for twenty-five years. Nevertheless, that was not the law's approach when it came to the duration of the payment if the wife did not remarry. It was not a "one size fits all" approach. Rather, it depended on how long they had been married.

What was the logic here? There wasn't any. There certainly was no logic when it came to how long the payment would continue if the wife did not marry. The legislature just picked the numbers out of a hat. And there was not even the pretense of any logic when it came to the payment ending in the event of the wife's remarriage. (Although the law was necessarily expressed in gender neutral terms, everyone knew that it was really directed at the wife.) It was based strictly on male chauvinism. The idea that a man could be obligated to make a payment to his former wife when someone else was enjoying her favors was just too much for men to swallow.

II

I am not suggesting that the framework I am going to recommend will solve all of the problems that husbands and wives will find themselves faced with if they divorce. It won't. Remember, the central theme of this series of books is that we cannot expect perfect solutions to imperfect problems. But it must be able to solve enough of their problems to enable divorcing husbands and wives who employ that framework to conclude an agreement.

With that in mind I want to divide the divorcing population into two groups. The first group consists of husbands and wives whose net worth, excluding the equity in their home, is not more than $30 million (again, in today's dollars). Why have I picked $30 million and not $20 million? After all, the majority of husbands and wives who get divorced, especially those who turn to divorce mediation, do not have a net worth of that amount. Because if they are going to divide their assets equally, as those in this group will, even if one of them (say the wife) does not work, she should be able to support herself adequately even without any contribution from her husband.

The second group consists of husbands and wives who have a net worth more than that. It can also include husbands and wives who, like Mr. and Mrs. Bezos, have a net worth that is far in excess of that. There is obviously another group as well, and that is the lower middle-class and the very poor, but since they do not normally turn to the law for help, we do not have to concern ourself with the law's effect upon them.

When it comes to the first group, the law should provide that their net worth should be divided equally—that equitable should be equal. When it comes to a maintenance payment, the amount, if any, should be based on need. (As I said, if one of them will be coming away with $15 million, they will not need to receive maintenance, regardless of what they earn. If they will be coming away with less than $15 million, they may or may not need such a payment, depending on their circumstances. Remember, this only applies to a maintenance payment. If there are infant children, their division of assets should have no effect on what would be an appropriate child support payment.

Though I didn't say this, when it comes to this first group, I viewed each of them as having one identity. They are a husband or a wife. But they could have two identities. They could also be an employed person. To be sure, it was not necessarily the case that both the husband and the wife had separate identities when our equitable distribution statutes were originally enacted—he usually did, she usually didn't. But it is far more often the case today. Just as important, while it might not be the rule, it is possible that her separate identity is more financially rewarding than his. And although our divorce laws have not and will not be amended to reflect that reality—which was one of the purposes of my proposed Copernican revolution in the law—that doesn't mean that it cannot and should not be reflected in what I have characterized as redefining the terms of the debate.

This brings me to the second group. Like those in the first group, those in the second group are going to "sit down and work it out." And they can work it out any way they wish. To be sure, they can base it on principle, as my good friend felt it should be—at least when he represented the wife. But I think that to do that represents a terrible distortion of our equitable distribution laws, and the fact that divorce lawyers endorse this doesn't make it any less of a distortion.

Our equitable divorce laws were not enacted to decide whether Mr. Bezos and Mrs. Bezos would be left with the same or different amounts to give away to charity. They were enacted to assure that, to the extent possible, they would each be left with what they needed, based on their previous standard of living. To be sure, it was argued, particularly by women's advocates, that divorcing wives were left at a distinct disadvantage in relationship to their husbands because women had forfeited their ability to advance their own careers by staying at home and raising their children. That was why a wife was entitled to receive an equitable share in the wealth that her husband had accumulated while they were married. Without her help he would never have been able to go out and become a captain of industry.

This, of course, was a fiction. It was also nonsense. Who cared? And what difference did it make? Not when it came to the first group. But it certainly made a difference when it came to Mr. and Mrs. Bezos. Was the only reason why Mr. Bezos had been able to build Amazon to where it is today because he had Mrs. Bezos by his side?

Think about it. When Picasso died, he left an estate of between $500 million and $3 billion in today's dollars, depending upon who evaluated the thousands of artworks that he had created which were part of his estate. Do any of us believe that Picasso would not have been able to create any of those art works had he not had whoever was his wife or paramour by his side—that she was the inspiration for all of it? It is a rhetorical question. Wasn't the same true of Mr. and Mrs. Bezos— and everyone else in that second group. In my terms, do our equitable distribution laws really apply to them? Did our state legislators really have them in mind when they enacted our equitable distribution laws?

To be sure, couples in that second group can "sit down and work it out" any way they want. But our divorce laws are not doing them any favor by making it harder for them to do that, which is the case when it is suggested that our equitable divorce laws should also be applied to couples in this second group. Ironically, though we may not be able to see and accept this currently, we will when more divorcing wives rather than their husbands are the ones who went out and conquered the world.

III

There is one final thing that needs to be said. In the two earlier books about divorce in this series, I argued that divorcing husbands and wives should make the decisions in their divorce the same way that they did in their marriage. Just as important, they should do so based on the same value system.

Lets start with the methodology. Suppose that they were not of one mind when it came to something during their marriage. How would you describe how they dealt with it? Just as I have. They didn't have a strict pre-determined procedure that they followed. Rather they just "sat down and worked it out." What yardstick did they use to judge the decisions they came to? They didn't use any. After all, the question wasn't whether they got it right. (Where did that idea come from?) It was whether they came to a decision. (In the terms that I have put it, whether they got it done.) But if the fact that they got it done was sufficient in their marriage, why isn't it sufficient in their divorce? It should be. It is just that the window dressing that our adversarial legal system and the divorce lawyers who are its agents have employed to sell their wares have disabled divorcing husbands and wives from being able to see this.

This brings us to the second and most important question. What value system should we employ when it comes to the judgment, if any, that we make about the decisions that they have come to? My answer was that we should employ the same value system that we employed in their marriage. Why would we employ any other?

With that in mind, I want to return to Chapter 13 in that previous book where I referred to an agreement that a husband and wife in a very long marriage concluded in mediation in which the husband got literally everything and the wife got almost nothing but which the wife nevertheless wanted to accept. The question I posed was not what the mediator should do (conclude the agreement for the parties or withdraw from the mediation), but what his attitude should be when it came to the wife's decision. My answer was that, in terms of our value system, it was none of his business. As he had not felt it was his business to pass judgment on the terrible price that the wife had been willing to pay all these years to stay married to this very poor excuse for a husband, it was not any of his business to pass judgment on the terrible price that she was willing to pay to get rid of him. After all, she could have stood up, walked out of the room, and gone off and retained the services of a divorce lawyer. None of us would have had any problem with that. After all, that was her decision. But she chose not to do that. And that was her decision as well.

Nevertheless, I knew that most of those who read that book would have a problem with that. From my standpoint that was their problem (and the mediator's) not the wife's or mine. Let me explain.

None of us object that when it comes to the judgments, if any, that we make with respect to the decisions that other people make in their lives, we do so on the basis of a value system that we subscribe to. And, as I said in Chapter 1 of *Divorce: Accepting Imperfect Solutions To Imperfect Problems*, that value systems necessarily involves compromises. Thus, if we do not wish to live in a world where committees of vigilantes go around knocking on our door to make inquiry and pass judgment on how we are conducting our lives, we accept the fact that we cannot go around knocking on our neighbor's door to inquire how they are conducting theirs.

What that means, of course, is that we do not make our decisions based on principle—on an inflexible rule that is applied uniformly to every judgment that we make. Rather, we judge each decision we make independently, on its own terms. At least that is what we do if we do not live in a world of possible perfection.

And that is the problem. As I have said over and over again, our Western philosophical and religious traditions are based on the assumption that we live in a world of possible perfection, and in that world principle rules. That is why a divorce lawyer could never accept the approach to the problem that I am recommending, namely, that when they turn to a divorce mediator who follows the roadmap that I am recommending, divorcing husbands and wives won't make their decisions based on principle, as my good friend did when he turned down the offer of $70 million made by the husband's attorney because it violated his principle that equitable means equal.

But if divorcing husbands and wives do not make their decisions based on principle, how will they make them? They will just "sit down and work it out." But, when they do that, what yardstick will they use to judge their decision? They won't use any. The fact that they have worked it out will be sufficient.

But what about the law? It is still there if it can be of any help. But it can't be of any help if it is employed, as a divorce lawyer does, as a weapon in a legal tug of war the object of which is simply to get as much as you can and to give as little as you have to. It can only be of help if it can be used as a common *framework* that divorcing husbands and wives can look to in their effort to conclude an agreement. But, as I hope this series of books has made clear, it is almost as if our divorce laws were designed to do anything but provide divorcing husbands and wives with a common *framework* that they could look to for that purpose. That is the sad legacy that our adversarial legal system and the divorce lawyers who are its agents have bequeathed to husbands and wives at this critical point in their lives. As I said, Shame, Shame.

CHAPTER 13

SUMMING IT UP

The first book on divorce in this series, *A Common Sense, Practical Guide To Divorce,* was thought out in advance in the sense that it represented my thinking about divorce over a period of more than 35 years. In fact, I had published it previously in an edition that included the Workbook which has now been published separately. On the other hand, the second book on divorce in this series, *Divorce: Accepting Imperfect Solutions To Imperfect Problems,* was an afterthought. In fact, as I have already acknowledged, I added Chapter 16 to that second book after I had already submitted it for publication.

This book was an afterthought as well, but in a very different sense. I literally made it up as I went along. But it was also the most difficult book that I have ever written, and time and time again I found myself confronted with a problem that I didn't think I could solve. At one point I even questioned whether I would be able to publish it. At another point I questioned whether I was asking too much of my reader. And the problems never seemed to end.

Why, then, am I publishing it? Because I came to believe that it was the most important book about divorce in the series. I also thought that it was a fitting end to the first book in the series, *The Book About Marriage: Entering It, Sustaining It, Ending It.*

But that still left me with a problem. Since I literally made it up as I went along, I never really set forth the essential themes in the book and, rather than leave my reader having to figure that out on his (or her) own, I thought that I owed it to him to indicate what they were. It is the purpose of this Summary to do that.

1. Though I argued in the first book on divorce in this series that the law should represent a "common framework" that divorcing husbands and wives could look to in their effort to conclude an agreement, when the three groups who most influenced the shape and content of our divorce laws—divorce lawyers, women's advocates, and the academic legal community—got through, our divorce laws were anything but that. Rather than answering their questions and solving their problems, the divorce laws that husbands and wives turned to for help had the exact opposite effect. They both left questions unanswered and created new problems for them.

2. To address that, I proposed what I referred to as a Copernican revolution in the law, one which would place a divorcing husband's and wife's efforts to conclude an agreement, rather than the law, as the center of their world. And in that world the question that our state legislatures would ask themselves was not whether the legislation they were considering would get it right, but whether it would enable husbands and wives who looked to the law for guidance to get it done. But as I came to realize, the three groups who had most influenced our divorce laws would never permit that. It wouldn't serve their purpose to do that.

3. But even if such a Copernican revolution took place, there were still two serious problems when it came to our divorce laws. The first was that they could not possibly shoulder all of the weight that was now being put on them. That was because the questions and problems that divorcing husbands and wives are faced with today are far more complicated than they were even 75 years ago, before the great increase in the rate of divorce took place. The second was that, in an important sense, the law

could only provide us with a "one size fits all" solution to the problem that literally didn't fit anyone. (I used the example of Mr. and Mrs. Bezos' divorce to make that point.)

4. If what I said was true, why have we not been able to see this? This brings us to Wittgenstein's famous saying about a picture holding us captive, which is a constant theme in this series of books. That picture more than anything else is what is getting us in trouble. The first thing that it does is hold us captive to the most unfortunate legacy that we have inherited from our Western philosophical and religious traditions, namely, the idea that we live in a world of possible perfection. We don't. On the contrary, as we are reminded every morning when we get up and leave our homes, we live in a very imperfect world, one of inevitable constraint and human limitation, and in such a world compromises will have to be made. Why? Because, as the second book about divorce in this series argues, it is not possible to have perfect solutions to imperfect problems.

5. There is a second aspect to Wittgenstein's famous saying about a picture holding us captive. In the context here it is not a picture that characterizes the law as representing simply a common *framework*—a neutrally charged characterization. It is a picture that characterizes the law as representing a divorcing husband's and wife's *legal rights*—a highly charged characterization. After all, the picture that holds us captive would literally have divorcing husbands and wives go to war if necessary to preserve their *legal rights*—in this case legal warfare. To avoid that, we could just as easily have characterized the law as representing the parties' *legal penalties*. After all, one person's gain is another person's loss. But characterizing it in those terms would not have served a divorce lawyer's purpose.

6. This brings us to the second most important message in the last two books about divorce in this series. That is the idea that I introduced in Chapter 16 of the second book on divorce, the chapter that I added as an afterthought. If divorcing husbands and wives cannot look to the law to solve all of their problems,

what can they look to? They can look to themselves. Regardless of what was and what was not the case 75 years ago, the reality is that people who marry today are assuming both a risk and a responsibility in the event that things do not turn out as they hoped and expected. Just as important, they are far better able to do that today, and that has to be factored into the equation. As I said, that is because the law is simply unable to bear the full weight of the consequences of their divorce.

7.   There is one last theme that has to be factored into the equation, and that is our value system. Although we are not consciously aware of this, we make many of our most important decisions based on the value system that we subscribe to, and in Chapter 1 of the second book on divorce, I summarized what that value system was when it came to the decisions that husbands and wives made in their marriage. That is because one of the central themes in the three books on divorce in this series is that we should subscribe to the same value system when it comes to the decisions that husbands and wives make in their divorce that we did when it came to the decisions that they made in their marriage. After all, don't their marriage and divorce take place in the same world?

Divorce lawyers do not accept this. On the contrary, they insist that divorcing husbands and wives must now make their decisions on the basis of a set of abstract principles derived from a transcendental world ruled by what is *fair* and *equitable*. Ironically, divorce mediators are guilty of the same thing, which is why I refer to them as simply divorce lawyers dressed in sheep's clothing.

Again, this is the point that I made in Chapter 13 of *Divorce: Accepting Imperfect Solutions to Imperfect Problems.* The value system that we subscribed to in their marriage accepted the fact that compromises would have to be made. Thus, if we did not want vigilantes knocking on our door to enquire how we were conducting our lives, we had to accept the fact that we did not have the right to knock on our neighbor's doors to do the same thing. By the same token, if we did not question the price that a wife had been willing to pay in the name of maintaining her marriage, who were we to judge the price that she was willing to pay in order to end it? After all, she had options there as well. She could hire a divorce lawyer and go to court. But that was her business, not ours. And instead of patting ourselves on the back for our Boy Scout good deed for the day, we should learn to mind our own business.

While the ostensible purpose of this Summary is to indicate the themes in this book, I want to expand upon that. On the face of it, the subject matter of this series of books is marriage and divorce. But that is not really the case. Its subject matter is life.

Let me explain. Contrary to what divorce lawyers would have you believe, your marriage and divorce are not separate from your life. They are part of your life and, as such, governed by the same influences, opportunities and limitations. That was certainly made clear in the book that preceded this one, *Divorce: Accepting Imperfect Solutions to Imperfect Problems*. After all, what was the central theme of that book? That we should subscribe to the same value system when it came to your divorce that we did when it came to your marriage. And what yardstick did we employ to judge the decisions that you made in your marriage? We didn't employ any? On the contrary, unless your decisions violated minimal societal standards (for example, deviated from the required child support payments), we didn't judge them at all.

But it went farther than that—much further. As I said, I was very consciously calling into question our entire Western philosophical and religious traditions, grounded in Plato's distinction between the everyday world of appearance and the real, transcendental world, which we gain access to by means of Reason. In doing that I was calling into question the appropriateness of the yardstick by which we were supposed to judge a divorcing husband's and wife's actions. Since there is no such transcendental world of Reason, there is no such yardstick. Thus, unless their proposed decision violated minimal societal standards, we should keep our hands in our pockets and mind our own business.

Again, if that is what we did in their marriage, that is what we should do in their divorce. Contrary to what divorce lawyers would have divorcing husbands and wives believe, our divorce laws are no more relevant because they insist on referring to them as representing their *legal rights*. After all, where has that gotten us when no two divorce lawyers ever agree what their *legal rights* are? As I said, it is just a game, and it is time that we stopped inducing divorcing husbands and wives to play it.

Addendum

A number of years ago, I wrote a book entitled *Divorce: The Conflict Between Getting It Right and Getting It Done*. Chapter 1 of that book started as follows: "It is generally accepted that, in terms of helping divorcing husbands and wives conclude an agreement between themselves, there are two equally important goals. Those two goals are to get it right and to get it done."

As I argued throughout that book, satisfying both of those two goals was complicated by the fact that, in terms of our adversarial legal system, divorcing husbands and wives had *conflicting interests*. What might be right for one of them might not be right for the other. The way that our adversarial legal system dealt with that problem was to insist that they each had to be represented by their own separate attorney—as our adversarial legal system put it, that given the fact of their conflicting interests it would be unethical for one attorney to represent both of them.

Therein lay the problem. A divorce lawyer didn't see his role to be to resolve the conflict between getting it right and getting it done. After all, he (or she), was an adversarial divorce lawyer and, as such, his obligation and goal was to get as much as he could and to give as little as he had to, and he looked to and employed the law for that purpose. The problem was that he could only do that if the law left him with sufficient running room by leaving him with a wide range of possible answers. And his opposing counsel felt the same way. The result was that when the parties two lawyers got through, they had made it harder, and in some cases impossible, to get it done, which was why it took them as long as it did to conclude an agreement.

Just the opposite was the case if the two of them turned to divorce mediation. The mediator in question was not an advocate for either of them. He (or she) was a neutral third party, and as such his primary goal was to get it done. And a narrow range of possible answers would serve him better. But what of the goal of getting it right? For a divorce mediator that was only a divorce lawyer's conceit. How could they possibly get it right if they turned to divorce lawyers when no two divorce lawyers ever agree what it means to get it right. To be sure, when all else fails, divorce lawyers can always turn to the court. But if they do that it will not be to get it right. It will only be to get it done.

But it is worse than that, far worse. It is not even possible to define what getting it right means. The polar opposite positions taken by a husband's and wife's divorce lawyers is proof enough of that. Moreover, for all of the reasons that I gave in book after book, it is a farce to suggest that turning to our divorce laws could possibly get it right, whatever that means. Turning to a coin would do as well. After all, unlike the application of the rules of mathematics, which are universal, our divorce laws vary from place to place and from time to time. That is why divorcing husbands and wives are inevitably left with a choice. They can go off and battle it out or they can sit down and work it out. And all of the rest is just talk.

I

This raises a question. Why is it so important to get it right? How did that become the object of the undertaking? When divorcing husbands and wives look back, they invariably have very different and conflicting views about their marriage. Why isn't the object of the undertaking to resolve that conflict and, in doing that, leave them with the right view of their marriage? Because they will never agree on what the right view is. To be more accurate, because there really is no right view of their marriage. To be sure, they will each have very strong feelings when it comes to this. But what would be the point of engaging in an endless, costly debate with respect to this if we know in advance that there is no right view, at least no view they will agree is the right one. Why not just leave it at that. After all, while they will never agree whether they got it right, they will know whether they got it done. To be sure, our adversarial legal system has blinded us to this by posing the issue as one of determining their *legal rights*. But that is only the "window dressing that a divorce lawyer employs to induce divorcing husbands and wives to engage in this pointless exercise. After all, since one person's gain is another person's loss, the object could just as easily have been characterized as determining their *legal penalties*. But that, of course, wouldn't sell.

What then is the answer? Up until this point the terms of the debate have been pretty much defined by our adversarial legal system which, to protect its turf, has posed the question as an ethical one based on what it refers to as the parties' conflicting interests. But, as I have pointed out time and time again, the parties also have interests in common, principal of which is not to allow what our adversarial legal system refers to as their conflicting interests to get so out of hand as to trump and do irreparable damage to their overall best interests by insisting that they go off and battle it out. To be sure, our adversarial legal system and the divorce lawyers who are its agents wouldn't understand what I was referring to when I talk about their overall best interests. But their overall best interests are no less important, or no less a casualty, on that account.

The distinction I have made is not simply an academic one. As I have argued, it has very practical and critical consequences. Rather than insist that they go out and battle it out, we would encourage the two of them to sit down and work it out. After all, isn't that what they did when they had a problem in their marriage. Isn't that what they would do if they did this completely on their own, which is what so many divorcing husbands and wives today are doing. Isn't that what Mr. and Mrs. Bezos did? And if that was good enough for them, why isn't it good enough for other divorcing husbands and wives? You don't need a law degree to understand this. Your common sense is enough to tell you.

This brings me to the title of this book, which sets as its object the purpose of redefining the terms of the debate. Until this point the terms of the debate have been between getting it right and getting it done. Where did we get the idea that it was possible to get it right? It was bequeathed to us by our Western philosophical and religious traditions which have insisted that since we live in a world of possible perfection, that is not only a realistic goal but the one to which we should direct our efforts. But, as we are reminded every day, we do not live in a world of possible perfection. On the contrary, we live in a very imperfect world, and in such a world we cannot expect perfect solutions to imperfect problems.

That is why divorcing husbands and wives have to choose. As I have posed it, they can go off and battle it out or they can sit down and work it out. And all of the rest is just talk.

CONCLUSION

I said earlier that I am not responsible for the world. I didn't create the world. I am only responsible for myself. But that doesn't mean that each of us isn't obligated to try to leave this place a little better than we found it.

As the result of a strange set of circumstances, I spent the last 50 years or more of my professional life wondering around in the world of divorce, first as a traditional divorce lawyer and then, for more than 35 of those years, as a divorce mediator. In that time, I had increasing discomfort with how our adversarial legal system and the divorce lawyers who were its agents were responding to the serious problems that divorcing husbands and wives came to them with. All too often they took what was already a tragedy in their lives and turned it into a nightmare.

While I felt that divorce mediation was a tremendous improvement, which is why I went into it, increasingly I had problems with it as well. That was because, as I put it, most divorce mediators were simply divorce lawyers dressed in sheep's clothing. To make matters worse, I increasingly had misgivings about both the quality and experience of those who were entering the field. There was certainly no requirement that they had to be lawyers. In fact, the leaders in the field took strong exception to that suggestion.

During this period of time, and starting with my third book, *Divorce Mediation: A Practice In Search of A Theory*, I tried to formulate what I felt was a more appropriate approach to the problem and, as the subtitle of that book suggested, to come up with A New Theory of the Law. The three books about divorce in this series represent the culmination of that attempt.

Having said that, I need to say one last thing. I am aware that in some instances I have somewhat simplified things in the sense of not addressing all of the possible considerations that could affect the decision. An example of that was defining the first group of divorcing husbands and wives as those whose net worth, aside from the equity in their home, was not more than $30 million. Why not $40 million? Because I was more interested in drawing a line than I was in determining where that line should be drawn. And I wanted the couple in question, not our state legislators or the trial judge who would hear their case if it went to trial, to do that. In most cases, the trial judge who will be assigned to their case will be anything but the smartest person in the room and you would be frightened at the thought of leaving the determination to him (or her) if you met him. As I said, if you would not have done that in your marriage, why would you do that in your divorce?

What was it that motivated my thinking when it came to drawing the line? It was practicality rather than principle. In the terms that I have put it, it was to focus on getting it done rather than on getting it right. In the terms that I have expressed it, it was to focus on what they need today and what they will need tomorrow, not on how much they will each be able to give away or leave to charity. And I wanted our divorce laws to give clear answers to that question and not, as is now the case, to base them on meaningless factors that are so ill defined that they don't leave divorcing husbands and wives with any answers at all. I appreciate the fact that it was more difficult to see this when the situation of divorcing wives was so different than it is today. And I am not suggesting that it is now a completely level playing field. It isn't. But it certainly is moving in the right direction. After all, Sheryl Sandberg did leave Facebook with $1.6 billion.

But there is another reason as well, particularly when it comes to divorcing husbands and wives who turn to divorce lawyers. It is not possible to define what getting it right means. It is as if it is a moving target. That being the case, it is pointless to hold out in the name of getting it right. But it is possible to get it done. More to the point, despite a divorce lawyer's deprecation of that goal, the fact that it is not possible to get it right makes getting it done even more important.

But it is important for another reason as well. Divorce is an emotionally difficult experience for many obvious reasons. One of those reasons is that it is very difficult for someone to come to terms with the fact that their marriage has ended in divorce and, from their standpoint, why—difficult for them to bring emotional closure to their marriage. Worse, for most divorcing husbands and wives they will not be able to do that unless and until they conclude an agreement—in the terms that I have put it, get it done. Nevertheless, if Mr, and Mrs. Bezos had not been able to sit down and work it out, the world would not have come to an end. What difference would it have made if it cost them $1 million in legal fees and two years of effort to finally get it done.

It would have made all of the difference in the world. Why? Because it would have taken them that much longer to bring closure to their marriage. That is why it is so important that divorcing husbands and wives are able to "sit down and work it out." Until they do, they are not going to be able to put this behind them as they would like to and need to.

I told you that, if you decide to follow the roadmap that I am recommending, you should pick someone who is smart. What I meant by that was that you should pick someone who knows what I have just told you and believes it as strongly as I do. But what I also meant was that you should not be taken in by what I have characterized as the window dressing that those who recommend a different roadmap have employed to get your attention. You will regret it. It is that simple.

I don't pretend that I have answered all of the questions or solved all of the problems that you are faced with as a result of your decision to divorce. But that was not what I set out to do. As I said, I am not responsible for the world. I didn't create the world. I am only responsible for myself. More modestly, the question is whether I have left this place a little better than I found it? That is not for me to say. Besides, only time will tell. But I would be lying if I denied that I am very proud of what I like to think was my contribution. Not bad for a no-account divorce lawyer from Garden City.

I said "what was my contribution" because I will be 90 years old on my next birthday and it is time for me to put down my pen and close my computer. I have been at this in one form or another for well over 50 years and that is a very long time.

I wish you well.

CPSIA information can be obtained
at www.ICGtesting.com
Printed in the USA
JSHW022047270922
31069JS00007B/182